Mary Carpenter

Reformatory Prison Discipline

As Developed by the Rt. Hon. Sir Walter Crofton

Mary Carpenter

Reformatory Prison Discipline
As Developed by the Rt. Hon. Sir Walter Crofton

ISBN/EAN: 9783744730051

Printed in Europe, USA, Canada, Australia, Japan

Cover: Foto ©Suzi / pixelio.de

More available books at **www.hansebooks.com**

REFORMATORY PRISON DISCIPLINE,

AS DEVELOPED BY THE

Rt. Hon. Sir WALTER CROFTON,

IN THE

IRISH CONVICT PRISONS.

BY

MARY CARPENTER,

Author of "Juvenile Delinquents," "Our Convicts,"
"Six Months in India," &c., &c.

LONDON:
LONGMAN, LONGMAN, GREEN, LONGMAN.
1872.

TO

MATTHEW DAVENPORT HILL, Esq., Q.C.,

LATE RECORDER OF BIRMINGHAM,

WHO,

FOREMOST OF ALL LIVING MEN,

HAS DEVELOPED ENLIGHTENED PRINCIPLES RESPECTING

THE TREATMENT OF CRIMINALS,

AND WHO,

BY HIS WISE COUNCILS AND SYMPATHY,

HAS STIMULATED AND AIDED THOSE ENGAGED IN

PRACTICAL WORK,

THIS LITTLE VOLUME IS RESPECTFULLY AND

GRATEFULLY DEDICATED.

PREFACE.

An INTERNATIONAL PRISON CONGRESS inaugurates a new era in our times.

The prisoner, removed from the view of society, and placed immediately under the governing powers, has been until recently cut off from our sympathies, and, as it has seemed, from the possibility of our helping him. His crimes alienated him from ordinary intercourse, and the world without has not ventured to intrude on the secrets of the prison house. HOWARD and ELIZABETH FRY revealed to the public the worse than unnecessary suffering which was inflicted on the wretched beings, who were incarcerated in abodes of vice and disease, and opened to them the doors of humanity. ROMILLY, MACKINTOSH, BROUGHAM, and others proclaimed new principles which should guide the treatment of criminals;—in the present day Mr. Recorder HILL in our own country, the Baron VON HOLTZENDORFF in Germany, M. DE MARANGY in France, with a few others, have steadily advocated reformatory principles. These have been practically developed by M. OBERMAIER in Munich, MONTESINOS in Spain, and MACONOCHIE in Australia;—these triumphantly demonstrated that the very worst men are capable of transformation into honest self-supporting members of society. Similar principles of action have produced similarly satisfactory results in the United States and elsewhere, in proportion as the means have been afforded for their free development. But these have been generally isolated exertions, depending for their success on individual efforts, and therefore not obtaining the confidence of the public, or the support of Governments. For the first time were all these principles embodied in a practical system in the Convict Prisons in Ireland, by the Right Honourable Sir WALTER CROFTON and his fellow Directors, with the support and sympathy of the late lamented Earl of CARLISLE, then Viceroy of Ireland.

During the last quarter of a century much attention has been paid by the legislature of our country to the principles of Prison Discipline. A Committee of the House of Commons in 1856 and the Royal Commission of 1856 established important principles, and laid valuable information before the public.

The subject of prison discipline is now felt of such importance to the general welfare of society, that governments in every part of the civilized world are sending representatives to the great Prison Discipline Congress which is about to assemble in London. They will carry back to the uttermost parts of the earth the results of experience, and the deliberations of those who have given attention to these important subjects. It is desirable that a clear and distinct account of the system developed by Sir WALTER CROFTON should be accessible to every one. The only complete account which exists, compiled from pamphlets and reports now inaccessible, is contained in the work, "Our Convicts ;"—this is now out of print. It is at the request of the United States Commissioner, Dr. WINES, to whom is due the original conception of this Congress, and its successful development, that this small work has been prepared.

RED LODGE HOUSE,
    BRISTOL, *May 1st*, 1872.

INTRODUCTION.

THE object of Prison Discipline is to transform offenders into honest self-supporting men and women, and eventually to minimise crime in society. Any system which effects these most desirable results, must be founded on sound principles; no mere mechanism, however excellent, can affect the moral nature of human beings; unless this is changed, no reformation can be real and permanent. It is, therefore, necessary to state the principles on which the Prison System established in Ireland by Sir Walter Crofton is founded, before entering on the development of it.

Let us first consider the actual state of the persons with whom we have to work.

Whatever may be the cause of their present condition, and however much or little they may morally be themselves to blame for it, the habitual offenders who constitute the largest proportion of the inmates of Convict prisons are in a state of absolute antagonism to society, and disregard of ordinances, human and divine. They are usually hardened in vice, and they concern themselves with the law only to endeavour to evade it. They dislike labour of all kinds, and to supply their own wants exert themselves only by preying on the property of others. They are self-indulgent,—low in their desires, ignorant of all knowledge that would profit them, skilful only in accomplishing their own wicked purposes.

But they are still men and woman, possessed of an immortal nature; still they are the children of the same Heavenly Father; still are they our fellow-citizens. They must not be wholly cast off from our sympathies, from our desire for their reformation.

To produce any permanent change in natures so perverted and hardened, it is evident that no merely external means can be of the slightest value. While under compulsory detention they may be bribed or terrified into some degree of quietude and submission, but their *natures* are not touched by these means. They return from the monotony and forced propriety of their prison life, only with fresh zest for the exciting career from which they have been for a season snatched. Their long abstinence from intoxicating stimulants is compensated for by increased excess. The hated forced labour of their servitude is at once abandoned for the wonted indolence of their old life. All who are acquainted with the histories of criminals, are well aware that this is the ordinary result of the ordinary imprisonment of Convicts, and hence arises a profound and general disbelief in the possibility of reformation, among those whose duties lead them to a knowledge of the "dangerous class."

A different principle of management produces different results, and does effect real reformation, provided all wise external means, which experience and sound judgment suggest, are adopted in developing the principle.

We shall now endeavour to ascertain what are the true principles of the treatment of Convicts, as individuals, and to show that these can be carried out in the legal punishment of criminals.

In the first place, the *will* of the individual should be brought into such a condition as to wish to reform, and to exert itself to that end, in coöperation with the persons who are set over him. The state of antagonism to society must be destroyed; the hostility to divine and human law must be subdued. This can never be done by mere force, or by any mechanical appliance. No fear of punishment, no hope of advantage, can produce a change of heart, or a true penitence towards God, and, without this, it is impossible that any reliable alteration in life can be effected. Severe suffering may subdue the will, and bring the individual into a state in which he may be more easily made sensible of his criminality towards God and towards man. But it is only when his heart is touched by the Christian sympathy of those around, when he can be made to understand that his own personal efforts alone can raise him,—that all that he is now enduring only has in view his restoration to society as an honest member of it; it is only then that he truly repents of his sins, humbles himself before his Creator, earnestly seeks divine help, desires to atone for his past misdeeds, is united to his fellow-beings by the bonds of Christian love, willingly accepts the discipline appointed for him, and gratefully works with those set over him for his restoration to society.

That such a change as this, proved by the future life to be a genuine reformation, has ever been accomplished, may be discredited by many, but is nevertheless true. And wherever such reformation has been effected, it will be found that the moving spring has been some person of large and Christian heart, who worked on principles founded on human nature, and on God's moral and revealed law; who framed a system in accordance with these, and carried it out with earnest purpose, enlisting in his work the hearts of those with him, because it was evidently good and true.

Whatever system can be proved to be most truly reformatory will, of course, be the best for society as minimizing crime to the greatest extent; it should therefore be introduced into legal punishment, as it will most benefit the public at large, as well as the individual. Yet, however firmly we may adhere to this reformatory principle, it is evident that we must not ignore or neglect another, viz., that it is the law both of God and of man that sin should be followed by suffering,—that what a man soweth that he must reap. These two principles are not opposed to each other, but are in perfect harmony, and if so worked will produce the best effects. How they may be harmonised has been thus set forth powerfully by Mr. Recorder HILL.

"The principles of secondary punishment may be reduced to three. First, the application of pain with the intention of proving to the sufferer, and to all who may learn his fate, that the profits of crime are overbalanced by its losses. This is the deterrent principle in action. The second principle is what BENTHAM calls that of *incapacitation*. So long as the criminal remains in gaol, society is protected from his misconduct, not by the deterrent operation of fear, but because he has for the time lost the power of offending. The third is the reformatory principle. Thus incapacitation deprives the malefactor of his power to do wrong,—deterrents overmaster by fear his desire for evil doing,—while by reformation that desire is extinguished, and is replaced by aspirations and habits which will furnish him with a safeguard against relapse.

/ "Now what is to prevent all these principles being combined in one and the same punishment. Reformation cannot be made the work of a day. It is a task which required a tedious length of time for its assured performance.")

Captain Machonochie effected probably the greatest triumphs of reformatory prison discipline ever attained, in Norfolk Island, in 1840. He transformed in three years into a well conducted colony, 1,480 doubly convicted prisoners, who were rigorously coerced all day, and cooped up at night in barracks which could not decently accommodate half that number. "A more demoniacal assemblage," he says,

" could not be imagined, and almost the most formid-
able sight I ever beheld, was the sea of faces upturned
to me when I first addressed them. I sought generally
by every means to recover the men's self-respect, to
gain their own wills towards their reform, to visit
moral offences severely, but to reduce the number of
those that were purely conventional, to mitigate the
penalties attached to these, and thus gradually awaken
better and more enlightened feelings among both
officers and men." Captain Maconochie thus stated
the principles on which he worked, in a pamphlet
published in Hobart Town, in 1839 :—

"The sole direct object of secondary punishment
should therefore, it is conceived, be the *reform*, if
possible, but, at all events, the adequate subjugation
and training to self command of the individuals subjected to them ; so that, before they can regain their
full privileges in society, after once forfeiting them,
they must give satisfactory proof that they again
deserve and are not likely to abuse them.   This
principle does not proscribe *punishment, as such*, which,
on the contrary, will, it is believed, be always found
indispensable, in order to induce penitence and submission ; nor, as may be already inferred, does it lose
sight of the object of setting a deterring example.
But it raises the character of both these elements in
treatment, placing the first in the light of a *benevolent
means*, whereas it is too often regarded as a *vindictive
end*, and obtaining the second by the exhibition of the
law *constantly and necessarily victorious over individual*

obstinacy, instead of frequently defeated by it. It cannot be doubted that very much of the harshness and obduracy of old offenders arises at present from the gratified pride of having braved the worst that the law can inflict, and maintained an unconquerable will amidst all its severities; and for this pride there would be no place, if endurance alone could serve no useful end, and only submission could restore to freedom.)

"The end *reform*, or its substitutes, sustained submission and self command, being thus made the first objects of secondary punishments, it is next contended that they can only be adequately pursued and tested,—first, by dividing the process employed into specific *punishment for the past*, and specific *training for the future;* and next, by grouping prisoners together, in the latter stage, in associations made to resemble ordinary life as closely as possible (in particular, sub-divided into smaller parties, or families, as may be agreed to among the men themselves, with common interests, and receiving wages in the form of marks of commendation, exchangeable at will for immediate gratifications, but of which a fixed accumulation should be required before the recovery of freedom), thus preparing for society in society, and providing a field for the exercise and cultivation of active *social virtues*, as well as for the habitual *voluntary* restraint of active social vices."

On such principles Sir Walter Crofton worked in the Irish Convict Prisons.

THE CROFTON SYSTEM.

——o——

CHAPTER I.

DESCRIPTION OF THE CROFTON SYSTEM.

THE system of Prison Discipline developed in the Irish Convict Prisons, by Sir Walter Crofton, while Chairman of the Board of Directors, is the only one known to exist in which all the principles have been fully developed, which have been already stated to be essential to the success of Reformatory Prison Discipline, and in which they have been carried into practical operation.

Every part of the system, even details apparently trifling, are essential to the successful working of the whole. It will therefore be attempted to present a clear account of the organization of every part of this system, and to show its intention and its connection with the whole. This will be derived from the various writings of Sir Walter Crofton himself.

B

The circumstances which led Sir Walter Crofton to the development of a truly reformatory system of Prison Discipline in Ireland must be borne in mind, in order to understand the bearing of some of its principles. In former times transportation was resorted to as the first secondary punishment. But our Colonists, with the exception of those of Western Australia, having refused any longer to receive our criminal population, it became necessary in 1853 to pass an Act of Parliament (16 & 17 Vict. c. 99) by which convicts under sentence of transportation could be discharged at home on "Tickets of License." We were thenceforward to provide in the United Kingdom for the liberation of convicts discharged from the Government prisons, with the exception of the small number which could at that time still be sent to Western Australia.

The British public having found that convicts at large on "license" were frequently in a most unreformed condition, felt increased unwillingness to receive into the labour market any who had on them the stigma of having been in gaol. The Irish Convict Prisons especially were known to be in a most unsatisfactory state. In order to prepare the way, thus, for the reception of the convict into society again in his own country, it was necessary that the discipline and training given in the prisons should be of a nature to inspire in the public a hope of the possible improvement of the delinquent, which experience had not hitherto led to ;—while such proofs of reformation, and such guarantee should be afforded, as to facilitate the absorbtion of the well-intentioned convict into the labour market.

Such were the two problems to be solved.

The grand difficulty, says Sir Walter,* consists in this :—"The convict comes to our custody in the great majority of cases an 'habitual criminal,' whose special vocation is that of crime. It is most important to note this statement. He has lived in antagonism to the law, and to all who carry out its biddings.

"This is the type of a very common case, with which, if we intend to avert a very serious social calamity, we are bound to grapple, if it is our object so to amend our criminal as to place him in the honest labour market at home, or in the colonies.

"Now this criminal must at the termination of his sentence return to the community either to live at the expense of others, or, by his own honest industry, if he can obtain employment and resist the snares of his antecedents. What, then, is the task before us?

> "1st. We have to punish him for the sake of deterring him and deterring others; but this will make him more hostile than ever. He has suffered mere penal infliction repeatedly, and has returned to prison more hardened than before. Punishment alone has failed to deter him.

---

* "Convict Systems and Transportation, 1863."

"2nd. We have to amend him; but how can this be effected with his mind in a state of hostility to us?

"3rd. We have to train him naturally before we liberate him, or the public will not value the voucher for his conduct; but how is this to be accomplished without the withdrawal of physical force?

"These were some of the difficulties which the 'Irish Convict System' had to encounter in 1854, and which very generally it was enabled to solve satisfactorily."

The simple principles which govern the system may be thus very briefly stated:—

"1st. That convicts are better and more reliably trained in small numbers, and by their being made to feel throughout their detention that their advancement depends on themselves, through the active exercise of qualities opposed to those which have led to their imprisonment.

"2nd. That the exhibition of the labour and training of the convicts in a more natural form, before their liberation, than is practicable in ordinary prisons, is a course obviously calculated to induce the public to assist in their absorption, and thereby to materially diminish the difficulties of the convict question.

" 3rd. That the institution of appliances to
render the criminal calling more hazardous
will assuredly tend to the diminution of
. crime ; and, therefore, that ' police supervision,' photography, and a systematic
communication with the Governors of county
gaols, with a view to bring, in all possible
cases, former convictions against offenders,
and entail lengthened sentences upon them,
are matters of the gravest importance, and
deserving of the most minute attention."

Under the guidance of such principles, we now
take our convict who has led a life of crime, is
hardened and defiant after various imprisonments,
and arrives at the prison in a state of absolute
antagonism to society. We desire to return him to
liberty penitent for his former offences, able and
willing to gain an honest livelihood. How is the
change to be effected ?

The system adopted may be briefly described as
follows :*—

" FIRST STAGE.

" Separate imprisonment in a cellular prison at
Mountjoy, Dublin, for the first eight or nine months
of the sentence. Whether the period is eight or
nine months, or even longer, depends upon the con-

---

* " A brief description of the Irish Convict System, 1862."

duct of the convict. If his conduct is quite unexceptionable, he would be entitled to be removed to an Associated Prison (the second stage) in eight months.

"In Ireland it is the practice to make this stage very penal, both by a very reduced dietary during the first half of the period—viz., four months—and by the absence of interesting employment during the first three months. By the time the convict is required for hard work in the second stage, the improved dietary in the later portion of the period in separation, will have rendered him physically equal to perform it; and by the end of three months of the first stage the idler will generally have learned to associate industry with pleasure.

"The convict learns something very material to his future well-being in the first stage—he has the advantage of much time devoted to his religious and secular instruction. He learns the whole bearing of the 'Irish Convict System' by means of scholastic instruction—that he can only reach the Intermediate Prisons (a special feature and a third stage in the system) through his own exertions, measured by marks in the second stage of the system. As the liberation of the convict within the period of his sentence depends upon the date of his admission to the Intermediate, or third stage, of the system, it is manifestly to his own interest, as it is the interest of those placed over him, that he should be well informed upon this point. There is a strong mental impression made consequent on this information.

" As the convict attains knowledge of the system, he feels that, within certain limits, he is made the arbiter of his own fate. Antagonism to the authorities placed over him gradually disappears, and in its stead arises a conviction that there is a coöperation where he had formerly anticipated oppression.

"The first stage will have done good work if it has succeeded in planting in the mind of the convict that there is an active coöperation existing between himself and those placed over him.

" At the end of eight or nine months, as the case may be, the convict is moved, if a labourer, to Spike Island Prison, to be employed on the fortifications, and if a tradesman, to Philipstown, to be employed at his trade.

"The Second Stage.

" The peculiar feature of the Irish Convict System in the second stage, is the institution of marks to govern the classification. This is a minute and intelligible monthly record of the power of the convict to govern himself, and very clearly realizes to his mind, that his progress to liberty, within the period of his sentence, can only be furthered by the cultivation and application of qualities opposed to those which led to his conviction.

" There are different classes to be attained in the second stage, and a certain number of marks are required to be obtained by the convict before he can be promoted from one class to another.

"The maximum number of marks each convict can attain monthly is nine, which are distributed under three different headings—viz., three for discipline, *i.e.*, general regularity and orderly demeanour; three for school, *i.e.*, the attention and desire evinced for improvement, or industry in school; and three for industry, *i.e.*, industry at work, and not skill which may have been previously acquired.

"There are four classes in the second stage—viz., the third (in which the convict is placed on his arrival from the first stage), the second, first, and advanced or A class.

"It will be possible for a convict to raise himself from the third to the second class in two months, by the acquisition of eighteen marks; from the second to the first in six months, if he has attained fifty-four marks in the second class; and from the first to the A or advanced class in twelve months, provided he has acquired 108 marks in the first class. When the convict has reached the A class his progress is noted monthly as A 1, A 2, &c. Misconduct causes reduction, suspension, or the loss of marks.

"When the convict attains the A class, he is employed (although still in the second stage of his detention) on special works, and kept apart from the other convicts. His school instruction and lectures take place in the evening.

"It will be intelligible, that the most successful in combating self, and in climbling the ladder of self-control and industry, will the soonest obtain the

, which
,'—and
ιpposod
ιe good
·eliance,
ing.
ιle and
ιl Sorvi-
3) how
wn fate.
o Inter-
ιe most
ι of the
ɔner has
conduct
Prisons
in this
ιing his
thereby
ɔn of a

attained
ι) before
risons is
heroforo,
ιt in the
n named
ιit of his
ho must
column)

"The rods of Imprisonment.

can attain
under three
pline, *i.e.*, {

	Shortest Period of detention in Intermediate Prsons.		Periods of Remission on License.
	YRS.	MTHS.	
three for se	0	4	
for improv			
for industi	—|—6		
which may	0	5	
"There	—|—3		
the third	0	6	The periods re-mitted on License will be proportion-ate to the length of sentences, and will depend upon the fitness of each Convict for re-lease, after a care-ful consideration has been given to his case by the Government.
arrival fror	—|—0		
advanced o	0	9	
"It wil	—|—6		
from the tl	1	3	
the acquis.	—|—3		
to the first	1	4	
marks in t	—|—0		
A or advai	1	6	
has acquir	—|—6		
the convict	1	9	
noted mont	—|—0		
reduction,	2	0	
"Wher	—|—0		
employed (			

detention)
other convi
take place
  "It wil
in combati
self-contro

Prisons apply only to those of the most will take place unless the Prisoner has the periods in the Intermediate Prisons ave the effect of postponing his admission extent the remission of a portion of his required number of marks, and the goal to which they lead—viz., ' The Intermediate Prisons,'—and thence the liberty, for which the convict is supposed to have been made fit, by the lessons of those good schoolmasters, industry, self-control, and self-reliance, succeeded by a very special and natural training.

" It will be seen by the appended scale and regulations for carrying out sentences of Penal Servitude under the Act of 1857 (20 & 21 Vict. c. 3) how much each convict becomes the arbiter of his own fate. The earliest possible periods of removal to Intermediate Prisons apply only to those of the most unexceptionable character, and no remission of the full sentence will take place unless the prisoner has qualified himself by carefully measured good conduct for passing the periods in the Intermediate Prisons prescribed by the rules; and any delay in this qualification will have the effect of postponing his admission into the Intermediate Prisons, and thereby deferring to the same extent the remission of a portion of his sentence.

" The class and number of marks to be attained by each convict (according to his sentence) before he can be removed to the Intermediate Prisons is shown in the first column. It is evident, therefore, that the time of detention of the convict in the Ordinary Prisons, within the minimum term named in the scale in the third column and the limit of his sentence, depends upon himself; and as he must pass a certain period (named in the fourth column) in the Intermediate Prisons before he can obtain his conditional liberty, the stimulus which he has to overcome self becomes very intelligible.

"Now, however trifling this 'Mark System' may appear to those not conversant with its operation, it will be found in practice to realize to the mind of each individual very clearly and fully his progress in self-government, and in other desirable qualities. There is not an intelligent officer in the Irish Convict Department who will not bear witness to the intense interest taken by each convict in the attainment of his marks, and the jealous care with which he notes them.

"THE THIRD OR INTERMEDIATE STAGE.

"In this stage there are no marks. The result of the self-discipline effected by their attainment is here to be tested before the liberation of the convict.

"'Individualization' is the ruling principle in these establishments; the number of inmates should, therefore, be small, and not exceed 100.

"The training is special, and the position of the convict made as natural as is possible; no more restraint is exercised over him than would be necessary to maintain order in any well-regulated establishment. At 'Lusk Common,' within fifteen miles of Dublin, there is an Intermediate Establishment for employing convicts in the reclamation of the land, and for carrying out principles which have proved so beneficial to themselves and to the public.

" The officers in the Intermediate Establishments work with the convicts.

" At 'Lusk' there are only six, and they are unarmed. Physical restraint is therefore impossible, and if possible, it would be out of place, and inconsistent with the principles which the establishments were instituted to enunciate.

" 1st.   You have to show to the convict that you really trust him, and give him credit for the amendment he has illustrated by his marks.

" 2nd.   You have to show to the public, that the convict, who will soon be restored to liberty for weal or for woe, may upon reasonable grounds be considered as capable of being safely employed.

" How does this become possible ?

" The reply is, that the convict is coöperating in his own amendment.   He cannot ignore the conviction, sooner or later, that the system, however penal in its development, is intended for his benefit ; and that moreover, it has by its stringent regulations and arrangements after the liberation of the convict, and this is most important to note, made the vocation of crime very unprofitable and hazardous to follow.

" He hears lectures of an interesting and profitable description, which not only point out the wickedness and the danger of criminal pursuits, but show him the course which he should take in order to amend his life, where his labour is required, and his antecedents not likely to entwine him to his ruin.

The mind of the convict is in alliance with the minds
of those placed over him, and what at first sight
might have appeared to be impracticable has become
for many years a recorded and gratifying fact.

"It is not averred that the mind of every convict
is, in these establishments, bent upon well doing,
but that the tone of general feeling is that of
desiring to amend, and is in the closest alliance with
the system.

"It is evident that this result is the attainment
of an enormous power, which it would be impossible
to secure by mere routine or mechanical appliances.

"The convict has felt the intention of the system,
the scope of which has been made clear to his mind—
that he is an individual whose special case and progress is noted, and very carefully watched in its
development."

In order to illustrate clearly the working and
influence of the system, Sir Walter takes a typical
case of a convict who is brought chained and scowling
to the prison, angry with all around him, and with
himself for not having been able to elude detec-
tion :—

"J. B. is stated to be twenty-eight years of age;
his life of crime has given him the appearance of
thirty-five. He is now convicted of burglary, and has
four former convictions recorded against him. He has
received what is termed a certain amount of penal
infliction for his different crimes, and has been on
the treadwheel more than once; solitude and dark-

ness also he has experienced from time to time. He has been violently insubordinate in prison, and has been flogged. He is known to be one of a notorious gang of robbers infesting one of our populous cities. You scan his countenance and there is not one hopeful lineament apparent. You elicit from him that his parents died in a workhouse, from which he absconded. He never had a home.

"How stand the public with regard to J. B?

"He must return to the community at the termination of his sentence either as J. B. the hardened burglar, to live on the industry of others; or J. B. the amended criminal who has resolved to live by his own honest industry, if he can obtain employment, and resist the meshes of his antecedents.

"J. B.'s sentence was fortunately long and in proportion to his criminal career. His prison conduct was for some time reckless and ungovernable; he defied the authorities and repudiated the marks which chronicled what he could not or would not obtain.

"Time, however, coupled with reflection and example, had worked a change in his case, as in that of many others; and although his misconduct caused his detention many years longer in the second stage than it need otherwise have been, before he could attain the requirement fixed for the Intermediate Establishments, he at last reached that goal.

"It was difficult to recognise J. B. scowling and defiant at all around him, in J. B. in the Inter-

mediate Establishment, cheerfully and willingly
giving his labour, after the ordinary hours, to save
the harvest for the State which had not only im-
prisoned him, but, in its strict requirement, had
detained him for years after his better-conducted
fellow-convicts.

"Why was this? The reason is plain. J. B.
was at last coöperating with those who were desirous
of amending him. He had realised, that the system which governed him, and under which he
had for some time struggled and suffered, was
innately just, although necessarily severe.

"J. B. has been employed since his liberation at
honest industry.

"There are many cases similar to that of J. B.,
although some greater and some less in degree.

"They would all, or nearly all, fail (humanly
speaking) if their sentences were of short duration."

Such is a general outline of the Convict System
developed in Dublin in 1854 under the auspices of
the lamented Earl of Carlisle, the late Viceroy of
Ireland. The full intention of the different parts of
the system was developed by Sir Walter Crofton in
his evidence before the Royal Commissioners on
Prison Discipline in 1863; from this the following
account is derived :—

"In Ireland this first stage is made very penal
by the omission of meat from the dietary for the
first four months. This was at first tried as an
experiment. It was my own opinion that the con-

victs had a larger dietary, when in separation, than was necessary for them. There might be some reason for giving them a better dietary when they were in association on the public works; but in separation it did not appear to me to be necessary. I called upon the medical officer to try an experiment for two months with an absence of meat from the dietary; he tried that experiment; and then I had another experiment tried for three months; and at last we attained four months; when I left Ireland, four months without a meat diet had been in use for some years. I am not at all persuaded in my own mind that four months need be the maximum for the absence of meat. My own opinion is, that if the convicts were given meat one month before they go to the associated labour prisons, it would be quite sufficient for them.

" The absence of interesting employment during the first three months is a feature which is peculiar to the Irish system. I will give the reasons as clearly as I can, and explain why the absence of interesting employment was necessary. What I mean by interesting employment is, the teaching of men trades when they come into the prisons. My observation was, that I found them all at work in their cells, learning shoemaking and all kinds of trades— and requiring, because very few of them in proportion were tradesmen, the attendance of the trades' warders to have constant intercourse with them, in order to obtain instruction. Now we have erected these prisons at an enormous cost for the purpose of creating, as I hope, depressing influences upon the minds of these men, before you work upon them in other ways. I felt that if they could converse, as they must converse in order to receive instruction, with the warders, during nearly the whole of the day, the warders coming backwards and forwards whenever they were required, the effect of the punishment of isolation would be very materially sacrificed. A change was made, and they were given, for the first three months, oakum to pick, and nothing else. To the public there could be no gain in trying to teach these employments, for what is done with these men afterwards? They were sent, nearly all of them, to the public works prisons—and these men were immediately to be made stonecutters and labourers, whom we had endeavoured to make cobblers at a sacrifice of material, and, still worse, of the depressing influences for which the prisons had been built.

"That in most cases a decidedly depressing effect was worked upon the prisoners by this treatment, in the first three months, at Mountjoy Prison, I have no doubt; and not only from my own observation, and from the observations of the governors and officers of prisons, but from information obtained from the convicts after their liberation ; a natural consequence I think of less diet and the absence of what I have called interesting employment, which had the effect of keeping the separation more distinct for a period of time. After three months, those who had been tradesmen, that is shoemakers and tailors, who did not require any special instruction, were set to work at their trades; others, who had no trade, were employed in mending the sheets of the prison establishments—in mending clothes, and in boot-closing, employments that do not require any supervision on the part of the officers; but they were not taught any trade.

"A prisoner during his stay at Mountjoy prison is one hour every day at school; but there is a great deal more taught him at Mountjoy than ordinary school instruction; he learns the whole scope of the convict system in Ireland; and when I say that he learns the whole scope of that system, it is an important matter that he should know everything that will be done with him with reference to his marks,—how his progress is recorded,—and how much depends upon his own exertions in every stage, to improve his position.

"This is made the subject of school lectures. The convicts are called up, and on a black board are required to illustrate the mark system, and to explain what will be done with them after they are out. They are made perfectly aware of the police arrangements of the country, and I am satisfied that these arrangements being impressed upon their minds at the commencement of their sentences, induces on their parts a feeling of coöperation with the system; they feel that they cannot pursue crime to the extent which they did formerly with impunity; and I am sure that this knowledge makes a very great impression on the general body of prisoners.)

"The maximum number of marks that each convict can obtain monthly is nine, but they are distributed under three different headings, namely, three for discipline, that is, for general regularity and orderly demeanour; three for school, that is, for attention and a desire for improvement or industry in the school. I should mention that it is not for a degree of attainment, but for industry in school. It is quite possible for an ignorant man, if learning his letters, to learn his letters industriously, and in that case he would get his maximum number of marks, while another man who could read very well perhaps would not get them; the marks are divided into three, two, and one, three being the highest under each head; three for industry, that is industry at work, not skill, which may have been previously acquired.

"The three heads are discipline, school and work. Now a convict must attain a maximum of marks during his detention to justify his obtaining a full remission of the term authorised by the regulations for the ticket-of-leave.

"This is the notice that is given to the convicts when they enter the prison *(handing in the same)*, and if a man does not accumulate enough marks in the time it is his own fault, and he is kept back till he does. Take the case of a man who is sentenced to three years' penal servitude, he must produce his document, and show that he is in the first class, with 90 marks made, before he can pass into the Intermediate Prison; if he has been longer than the usual time in attaining them, he would not come into the Intermediate Prison until later, but that would be his own fault and not ours; he must then remain a certain time in the Intermediate Prison in proportion to his sentence, and therefore it not only delays his coming into the Intermediate Prison, but it postpones his obtaining his ticket-of-leave. A proportion is laid down for each sentence, and when you examine the sentences you will find the number who have been sent out on tickets-on-leave, and the periods of remission will show how this system has worked. I should also explain the classes in the stages; there are four classes in the stage at Spike Island, the third, the second and the first, and the advanced or A class. This class was called 'exemplary' for two or three years, but we thought that the term exemplary was not very applicable to convicts, and it is now called the advanced class. It is possible for a convict to raise himself from the third class to the second class in two months. When they leave the separate prison they go into the third class; they begin low down in that class, on the ground that in separation there is little opportunity of doing much amiss; it does not afford the same test as the other prisons. It would be the highest number of marks attainable (18) by a convict that would get him from the third to the second class in two months. He

could get from the second to the first class in six
months, provided he attains 54 marks in that period ;
nine is the maximum for a month ; if not attained,
the convict gets delayed in each class before he is
moved, in consequence of this want of marks telling
against him ; then he can get from the first to A or
the advanced class in 12 months, provided he has
attained 108, that is nine marks a month, 12 times
nine making 108. When a convict has reached the
A class his progress is noted, as A 1, A 2, and so on ;
any misconduct causes a reduction and suspension or
a loss of marks.

"A convict has no gratuity in separation, but he
has 1*d*. a week in the third class, 2*d*. a week in the
second class, and 3*d*. and 4*d*. in the first class, which
is divided. That is reserved for the convict to
receive when he goes out of prison. It is from 7*d*.
to 9*d*. in the advanced or A class. Now I will call
the attention of the Commission to the lowness of
the gratuities in this system, because it is considered
that the convicts should have a long up-hill career
for some time as a test. The Directors believe them
to be thus better tried before they give them a higher
gratuity, which I shall explain when I come to the
Intermediate Prisons. In the 3rd class it is 1*d*., in
the second class 2*d*., and in the third class 3*d*. and
4*d*., and in the advanced class it is from 7*d*. to 9*d*.
Taking the whole of the gratuities in the Intermediate
Prisons, and all other prisons, the average amount
of the gratuities in Ireland is about one-half of what
it is in England.

"When men attain the A class or the advanced class in that stage, they are moved, by the system, to another part of the establishment, and are employed on special works; the men who are idlers are kept by themselves in a class. The men who are dangerous are kept by themselves also, and withdrawn altogether from the general labourers of the prison. They are subject to very strict treatment; for instance, the idlers, who do not do their work and interfere with the general class, are put by themselves and employed, with very little food; the dietaries are altered especially for them.

"There is another class of men who assault the officers—violent men—who are kept in what is called the dangerous class. They are kept in chains to prevent them doing further mischief, and also only upon such dietary as the medical officer thinks is absolutely necessary for them; but it is very low.

"There is a class of dietary for the idlers, and a class for the dangerous men, and they are kept perfectly separate; their dietary is reduced until they show, by their future conduct, that they deserve to be put in the ordinary labour classes. Now, I attribute to this minute classification of these men, the being able for the last three and a half years to do without flogging, although I may add that I have no objection to find flogging retained as a punishment. *We have not resorted to it during the last three and a half years*, proving, I think, that this kind of classification, under stringent rules, is very advantageous; it is satisfactory to know that although at the commencement there were several in these classes, very few are in them now.

"I can record from actual experience that the marks are of the utmost value; that they are the means of acting upon a man as an individual, and of realising to him his own position and his own means of progress; I know of no other way in which you can equally produce that effect upon him. I am quite satisfied that wherever the system of marks is tried it will succeed.

"There are four persons who are connected with the appointment of the marks; viz., the officer of the gang, the schoolmaster, the principal warders, and the governor; and with regard to the convict, he has the means of seeing the director as to anything which he believes to have been unjustly noted against him.

"I have already called attention to the advanced class; the moment that a man attains a position in that class he is put into a detached portion of the prison, and kept there under a different system. That class have their meals and work together, they are employed on special works at Haulbowline, and have more work, because they have school in the evening; they are dealt with specially in every way; the 1st, 2nd, and 3rd are worked together. They are in a distinct building."

This advanced class terminates the ordinary prison discipline, and leads on to the Intermediate Prisons, of which an account will be given in the following chapter .

CHAPTER II.

THE INTERMEDIATE PRISONS.

WE have now described the actual machinery adopted in the Convict Prisons as organised by Sir Walter Crofton. This well devised system would, however, have had little effect if it had not been based on sound principles of reformatory action, and on a deep knowledge of human nature. All these are skilfully blended in the Crofton System so as to form a perfect whole, and to influence the convict from the first moment when he enters the gaol. He is taught by the circumstances in which he is placed, as much as by direct instruction, that he has sinned against God and man, and must suffer for his evil doing, but that this suffering is not inflicted on him from vindictive feeling, but as a solemn duty, and with a view to his ultimate restoration to society. He is led on stage by stage, to higher degrees of improvement, physically, intellectually and spiritually, and gradually learns to feel that all advancement depends on his own personal efforts, he thus at length reaches a position in which he may be regarded as fit to be discharged and restored to society. But what guarantee has the public that he is really reformed? How can he himself be certain that he can safely encounter the temptations of the world, from which he has been hitherto shielded by the prison walls? Though he may have had as great a degree of liberty as was consistent with gaol discipline, yet his will has been still restrained, he has been surrounded with appliances to help him to do right and stimulated with inducements to self-controul;—how can the public feel a confidence that when these are removed he will be proof against temptation? How can he be sure of himself? A profound distrust exists, and with just reason, in the public mind of good "prison character." How can reformation be proved to be real, and how can society be so satisfied that it is so, as to be willing to receive convicts into their midst and absorb them into the labour market? Such perplexities occurred to Sir Walter Crofton, and his fellow directors, Captain Knight and Mr. Lentaigne, gentlemen who fully entered into the spirit of the undertaking, and brought their own special qualifications and experience to bear upon it.

A year's experience brought the Directors nearer to the solution of their grand difficulty. They say in the Second Report, p. 23, "We are of opinion that the employment of convicts, selected on account of their general good conduct, &c., in small bodies on public works in various localities, under circumstances of exposure to the ordinary temptations and trials of the world, when the reality and sincerity of their reformation may be fairly and publicly tested, will present the most favourable chances for their gradual absorbtion into the body of the community."

This is of course the grand object which, if attained, may be considered the crowning success of all prison discipline. As we proceed, year by year, we shall find this idea steadily kept in view by the Directors, until at last society had become so willing to re-admit to the labour market the former culprit, who had given reliable proof of repentance, and of a desire and an ability to lead a new life.

" We hope," continue the Directors, " by means of a careful selection of convicts, according to their general, as well as ' prison character,' by their employment in small bodies in various localities, comparatively as freemen (though under surveillance) that the public will gradually become convinced of the difference to which we have alluded, that many of these men are not utterly irreclaimable, and that by degrees they will become willing to extend a helping hand to such as may really prove themselves deserving of their aid and encouragement. We believe that a general desire is felt by the community at large to aid in the restoration of these fallen members of society, though all, or nearly all, shrink from personal contact with them."

Before proceeding to give an account of the way in which this object was carried out in the Intermediate Prisons, which are the peculiar feature of the Crofton system, we must present some idea of the difficulties which had to be overcome in the introduction of the system, and the manner in which these were surmounted.

The Directors entered on their work with a full knowledge of the difficulties they would have to encounter. "We anticipated," they say, p. 4, "that on the commencement of the new system, whilst in a transition state, both as regards officers and prisoners, many subjects of jarring disappointment and discontent would be likely to arise and cause troubles in the prisons; this was the case to some extent, and called for the exercise of great discrimination and firmness on the part of the local prison authorities. We regret to state that many violent and turbulent offences having occurred in the early part of the year, it became necessary to resort to severe punishments, which, however, were carefully watched by the medical officers; these occurred principally during the disorganization of Philipstown Prison. We are happy to state, however, that the system is now thoroughly understood and appreciated by officers and prisoners, who are aware that, although the evil disposed will assuredly receive the treatment their conduct merits, those who have chosen a different course will meet with every encouragement."

The Directors perceived that it was essential to the success of their work to raise the convicts from their very low and degraded intellectual condition; they know that this was no easy task, and that it was

not sufficient to establish schoolmasters in the gaols,
unless they took other measures both to stimulate the
teachers, and to rouse to exertion their very ignorant
scholars. They thus speak in the same report of the
steps they took, p. 3 :—"In our last report we com-
plained of the inefficient state of the Educational
Departments of the Convict Depôts, and stated the
importance we conceived should be attached to them
in this country, recommending at the same time that
they should be placed under the Inspectors of the
National Board of Education. Experience has proved
that we were correct in our opinion ; the report of
Mr. M'Gauran, the head schoolmaster at Mountjoy
Prison, shows, that after a very careful examination
of the prisoners at that establishment, he found that
96·2 per cent. were almost without any education at
all ; a fact, we submit, calling for every exertion to
render the educational machinery as perfect as possible,
in order to open the minds of the prisoners, by a
system of training as well as teaching."

Having then somewhat prepared the way, the
Directors established intermediate stages at Smithfield and at Forts Camden and Carlisle for convicts
who had passed through the "advanced class."
Here the Mark System was discontinued ; increased
responsibility and liberty being themselves the great
reward ; this stage was the last before actual freedom, and to retain his place in it the convict must
prove by his diligence, his efforts at self-controul,
and discharge of duty, that he is fit for it.

The Directors thus speak of the result in their third report :—"Generally speaking, the industry of the convicts has been very satisfactory, especially of those in the Intermediate Stages at Smithfield, and at Forts Camden and Carlisle. *The record of industry being known to affect their progress in the advantages of classification* has been a constant stimulus, which we hope will become still more powerful with the men now under sentence of penal servitude, when we are entitled to place before them some more tangible reward than is afforded by the mere increase of earnings, consequent on their attaining higher classification."

The physical effect on the prisoners of the change of treatment adopted in the Smithfield Intermediate Prisons, is strikingly shown in the following extracts from the report of the medical officer, Thos. Brady, Esq. These results are the more remarkable because they occur in cases where the preceding injurious condition may have left, and probably did leave, very injurious effects on the constitution :—

"Any one conversant with the medical statistics of Convict Prisons in Ireland will see from the preceding hospital returns alone that the sanitary state of the prison during these eleven months was very satisfactory, and indeed exceptional. This becomes more manifest, however, when we consider that all the prisoners in confinement here (251) had previously undergone long periods of confinement, varying from three and a quarter to six years, and hence belonged to the class of convicts enfeebled by long confinement, among whom the serious illness and mortality of former years chiefly occurred. It is true they were a select class of such prisoners, but very few of them were strong, many were delicate, and all bore the traces of long confinement, and moreover they were constantly employed at such trades as shoemaking, tailoring, mat making, &c.; and worked more steadily and assiduously than the convicts here at any former time.

"But the sanitary state of the prison was in reality more favourable than could be inferred from any mere numerical results, and was most remarkably manifested in the character of the sickness that prevailed. I would not attach undue importance to the *total absence of mortality,* which was probably an accidental circumstance; but what was really remarkable and significant, all the diseases of the period occurred so much modified and mitigated in character and form, as clearly indicated that the health of the prisoners was sustained by some peculiar sanitary influence." * * * "*This improved sanitary state of the prison dates from the introduction of the reformatory system ; and, in my opinion, is attributable to the agency of several concurring salutary influences which this system brings to bear upon the criminal, and which produce as remarkable an improvement in the mental and moral condition, the temper, feelings, character and conduct of the prisoner, as in his general health. In whatever circum-*

stances the prisoners here are observed, this improved
state of feeling is very apparent. In the workshops
it is manifested in the cheerfulness, alacrity and
assiduity, with which they apply themselves to their
laborious occupations, and furnishes a striking con-
trast to the listlessness, sullenness and gloom, so
commonly exhibited by the ordinary convict in similar
circumstances. In the school, the earnestness and
vivacity with which they engage in their studies
after the fatigue of the day, and the anxiety they
evince to acquire information and excel one another,
afford still more satisfactory evidence of mental and
moral improvement; though at the same time it
must be acknowledged that much of this was attributable to the agreeable and skilful manner in which
instruction is imparted to them in this prison, by
lecturing, diagrams, maps, &c., and to the judicious
selection of subjects suited to their capacity, and
supplying the kind of information which is attractive
and interesting to persons in their condition. In the
hospital, also, an improved state of feeling has been
equally manifest. It is a common practice among
the convicts to endeavour to get into hospital, or to
remain there after they are perfectly recovered, in
order to avoid the prison duties; *very few cases of
this kind have occurred under the new system.* Another,
and by no means unfrequent occurrence observed in
the Convict Prisons, and more especially among the
prisoners whose health has suffered from long confinement, and who have been anticipating their

approaching release from prison, is that when the prisoner is attacked with any serious disease he is at once prostrated in body and mind, comes into the hospital with the gloomy foreboding that he will never leave the prison alive, and lies down, as it were, to die, hopeless and desponding, thus rendering all the resources of art unavailing. A very different spirit prevailed among the prisoners here since the change of management took place. In fact, they appeared to me, in most cases, rather disposed to underrate the seriousness of their sickness, and to rely too much on their improved health, and were only anxious and eager to return to those duties which have ceased to be distasteful to them.

"Those who have had opportunities of observing the powerful influence, for good or evil, that mental feelings and emotions, hope and joy, grief and despondency, exercise upon the human body in sickness and in health, as well as in the world outside, as within the walls of a prison, will have no difficulty in comprehending that this buoyant state of mind and hopeful spirit of the prisoners must have largely contributed to produce the improved sanitary condition of the prison during the past year.

"It is almost unnecessary for me to observe that with prisoners in this state of mind, remunerative labour and the acquisition of interesting and useful knowledge in the school are, in themselves, sanitary influences of no slight importance.

"Indeed this system of treatment may be

regarded as not only reformatory but sanitary to
the prisoner, and is brought to bear on him at the
period of his imprisonment when he most needs it;
so that he is, as it were, prepared, as the period of
his liberation from prison approaches, to return to
society in such a state of health as will enable him
to make good use of the skill and information he
has acquired in confinement."

The experience of six years only confirmed the
testimony here borne to the results on the prisoner of
the system adopted. Mr. Brady writes (May 4,
1863):—

"I have great pleasure in being able to assure
you that the remarkable improvement which took
place in the sanitary state of the convicts in the
Intermediate Prisons, on the establishment of the
reformatory system, has been fully sustained ever
since.

"The diseases that have occurred, without almost
an exception, have been of a simple character and
mild form, such as might occur in any family, and
requiring merely a few days' residence in hospital
for their cure.

"I have observed that the prisoner begins to
improve in health from the moment he passes the
threshold of the Intermediate Prison, even though
he be weakly and shattered by previous confinement,
and in most instances his improvement in health is
so rapid as to excite the astonishment of those who
have seen him at the time of his admission. I may

observe that the facts stated here have been repeatedly put forward in my annual reports."

The following description of the Smithfield Intermediate Prison was contributed to "Once a Week" by a member of the Social Science Congress, which met in Dublin in the summer of 1861 ; it gives a distinct idea of the plan and system pursued :—

"Smithfield is an old prison of the ordinary kind, which, being at liberty, has been adapted to its present purpose, while still retaining the cellular arrangement for sleeping. With this exception there is scarcely anything to remind one of a prison. The workshops, the large simple dining-room, used also for evening lectures and other instruction ; the cheerful open yard for exercise, enlivened by small garden plots—all would give one rather the idea of a model lodging-house with associated workshops, than anything of a penal character. The men were at dinner when we arrived, and we requested permission to see them at their meal. As we approached the dining-room we heard the sound of cheerful orderly conversation ; and, on entering, found to our surprise, that there was no superintendent present, but that the prisoners were conducting themselves with as much propriety as ordinary workmen. They have not even separate rations weighed out to them, but the whole fixed quantity of food being placed on the table, they help themselves with due regard to each other's rights. Those who know what care is usually necessary in prisons, workhouses, and even schools, to give to each inmate the exact portion of food appointed, in order to prevent dissatisfaction, will appreciate the admirable tone of feeling which the possibility of such latitude indicates. The men appeared somewhat embarrassed by our presence, and perplexed at what could be the motive of such a visit ; we therefore requested to see their library, and one of their number, the librarian, showed us with much pleasure a good collection of useful and interesting books, to which they have free access, purchased partly by the contributions of the prisoners themselves.

"It was Sunday ; and after a little friendly intercourse among themselves in the court, the Catholics and Protestants separated into different rooms, where their respective chaplains gave them an afternoon's religious lecture. We meanwhile gained much information from the Superintendent respecting the system adopted : he objects to being designated Governor, desiring that the prison tone should be as much lost sight of as possible. Captain Crofton was not with us on this occasion, which was on the whole better, as we saw everything in its ordinary condition, without the controuling influence of his presence. Yet his absence only made us more completely perceive how much his spirit pervades the whole. The Superintendent seemed thoroughly imbued with the Captain's principles of management, and spoke in warm terms of their effect on the men. Though all regulations are very strictly carried out, yet, as the prisoners feel

that everything is ordered with a regard to their real
welfare, and administered with perfect justice, they
work with their superiors, instead of against them,
as is so commonly the case in prisons; their wills are
enlisted, and there is very seldom any cause of complaint. On several occasions some of the men have
been employed at work at the prisons in the city at
some distance : no difficulty has ever been experienced
in marching them to and fro through the crowded
city, with a single officer. Some of the men who are
the nearest to their final discharge are even permitted
to go alone into the city, to carry messages, or to
execute commissions. The prisoners are allowed, if
they choose, to spend sixpence a week of their earnings in any innocent indulgence; they intrust with
the purchase these privileged messengers, who have
never been known to be unfaithful to their trust. A
man who had been thus sent out on the preceding
day was summoned, and gave us an account of three
several expeditions of the kind. The time is of
course exactly noted when they go out and return,
and the messenger knows that any neglect of duty
would be certainly discovered and would entail on
him serious consequences. Still the moral controul
appeared to us astonishing, which should be more
powerful than bolts and bars on one so low and
degraded as a convict! They *had been* convicts,—
they were treated as *men;* they had been made
to feel that they were men not for ever degraded,
but who might resume their place in society, or

even take one, if they had never yet been regarded
as other than outcasts. They comprehended the
position in which they were here placed, as men
who might be trusted; and they proved themselves
worthy of it.

" The lecture ended, we were invited to be present
at a 'competitive examination,' which usually takes
place on Saturday evening, but which had been
deferred for our benefit. Mr. Organ, the lecturer to
the prison, gives the men evening lectures on subjects
calculated to communicate such knowledge as may
be advantageous to them in their future life, besides
storing their minds with useful information, and
drawing them off from improper subjects of thought.
He is much more than a lecturer; he is a friend in
the highest and best sense, to those who, perhaps,
never before had a friend worthy of the name; he
sympathises with their difficulties and trials; and
when they are about again to enter into the world, he
arranges for their emigration if they wish to leave
the country; does not fear to advance them for the
purpose, from his private purse, the money which
will be afterwards paid to them for their earnings,
and in every way in his power promotes their true
interests, and literally gives himself, his time, his
strength, his heart, to the objects of his anxious care.
In doing so he has had the warm sympathy, not only
of Captain Crofton and the other prison Directors,
but of the Lord-Lieutenant, Lord Carlisle, who has
even honoured with his presence some of these

evening lectures, and has bestowed on him in his difficult and trying work that friendly encouragement which is more precious and supporting than any other human help.

" Mr. Organ gave the men on the present occasion one of his forcible familiar addresses, and their countenances clearly indicated how completely he touched their experiences. We had now a good opportunity of studying the characters before us. Some were grey-headed men, evidently ignorant and stupid, if not hardened in crime ; some quite young, perhaps only eighteen ; the countenances of some were not unpleasant, and had evidently been greatly softened and refined by the discipline they had undergone, while the bulk of them were certainly unprepossessing, though not bad, and were responsive to good sentiments or advice. One would not have imagined oneself in such an assemblage—all convicts of a deep dye. Those of us were particularly struck with this, who had elsewhere seen so very different an aspect in a number of convicts in other prisons, where the hard, dogged, lowering look gives unmistakeable proof of a bad nature checked and repressed, not changed. After the address, the men arranged themselves in two parties, and a man on one side was selected to propose a question to the other. This being satisfactorily answered, the challenge was returned, and each side seemed stimulated by a friendly rivalry to surpass the other, to elicit as much information and call out as much real thought and opinion as possible. Sometimes a discussion arose, in which Mr. Organ was called on to take a part, which he did, not dictatorially, but with only the superiority arising from his own greater knowledge and better spirit and judgment.

"Leaving the prisoners with a few words of encouragement and exhortation, we were taken to an outside waiting-room, where were a number of men who, having been set at conditional liberty, came to report themselves as steadily at work, and others who had been for many years free, but who kept up this occasional connection with those who had laboured for their good. These results of the labour and care bestowed were most satisfactory; and still more so were the visits made by some members of the Social Science Congress to employers who had many of the late convicts at work under them, and who spoke highly of their reformed condition.

"We paid another visit to Smithfield with Captain Crofton, and saw the men at work at their several trades. A certain proportion of the profits is allowed them, so that a good workman may earn his 2s. 6d. a week, which is laid by for his discharge, except the few pence which he is allowed weekly to spend."

The grand triumph, however, of Sir Walter Crofton's System of prison discipline is Lusk Common. The convicts are within walls at Smithfield, though with as great an amount of liberty as was possible under the circumstances. But now their power of self-controul was to be exposed to an even severer test,—they were to have nothing to confine them but *la chef des champs*, as Demetz terms it,—they were to be placed in the midst of an open country with nothing to prevent them from absconding, and thus forfeiting the position they had gained,—but their own resolute will. The experiment appeared so dangerous that no one believed that the thing could be done, except Sir Walter. He received multitudes of anonymous letters warning him to abandon his project;—the convicts themselves did not believe in their own possibility to resist such a temptation. But he was firm. Nothing shook his confidence in his principles. He himself accompanied out the first small party of convicts and their officers. They looked wistfully at him as he departed, and evidently feared the worst. With some very natural anxiety he went early to visit his young institution. Everything was safe! Lusk was established! The following account of it is derived from a work published in the autumn of 1861, by four Yorkshire magistrates who visited it :—

"Lusk is a village about twelve miles from Dublin. Powers were obtained by Act of Parliament to enclose an open common there, previously occupied only by 'squatters.' Two huts of corrugated iron, each capable of holding fifty men, were erected at a cost of £320 a piece. A portion of each hut is partitioned off for a warder to sleep in, and the rest serves both as day-room and dormitory for the convicts. A cook-house and offices of the simplest

possible character, stand, with the huts, in an enclosure bounded by a mud wall a yard high. A few
cottages for warders scattered about the common,
complete the whole *matériel* of the 'prison.' All the
usual features of a prison may be said—with something of the idiom of the country, though not without
high English authority for ihe phrase—to be 'con-
spicuous by their absence.'

"As to the *personnel,* we found at the time of our
visit about sixty convicts in charge of five warders.
The truncheons we saw at Mountjoy, have no place
here, and other weapon or chain there is none.

"The obvious question to ask first is—Do not the
prisoners often escape ? Of more than a thousand
men, we are told, who have passed through the
prison, only two have attempted it.

"There is a military guard ? No. There are
police ? The answer is instructive. When the
establishment at Lusk was first proposed, the resi-
dents in the neighbourhood were, not unnaturally,
somewhat alarmed at the idea of having a number
of thieves and burglars encamped in open quarters
near them. To calm these apprehensions, it was
proposed that the constabulary should have a station
on the common. An iron hut which had been erected
elsewhere was brought and set up for the purpose.
But no police ever came, for there has never been
found the slightest need for them. We were assured
by Mr. Cobbe, a magistrate having large property,
and himself resident within a few miles, that so

unexceptionable has been the conduct of the prisoners, that he has never heard any complaint whatever of misconduct on the part of the prisoners, either within the establishment, or outside.

" Is, then, the non-escape of the prisoners owing to the place being made so comfortable to them that they have no wish to leave it? We certainly failed to find any evidence of such comfort. The men sleep in hammocks in the hut, and all that one can say is, that while they are inside it, they have shelter; but the moment they leave it, they are exposed to every wind of heaven, and to all the rain of that humid climate. In point of mere physical comfort, the advantage is altogether on the side of an ordinary prison, to say nothing of a well-warmed cell at Wakefield or Pentonville. We found most of the men, at the time of our visit, working up to the middle in drains, than which few employments conduce less to comfort. The diet is stated to be not more than the medical officers consider to be necessary for the maintenance of health, and fitness for the hard labour and exposure to which the men are subjected.

" The gratuity is half-a-crown a week, which is rather more than in any one stage at Portland. But it is so much lower in all the previous stages, that a convict, under a four years' sentence, in Ireland, can only earn half the amount which he could earn, under a similar sentence, in England.

" The men at Lusk are allowed to spend sixpence

a week of their gratuity; and we were told that many of them buy bread with it,—an indication that the diet allowed to them is not excessive.

"On the whole we saw no appearance of any indulgence to induce men to remain, as they do, without physical restraint, and submit to strict discipline.

"We have mentioned one independent source, from which we heard of their general good conduct. Another was the rector of the parish, who informed us that the Protestant prisoners attend service at the village church, and conduct themselves with as much propriety as any others of the congregation.

"The aspect of the men whom we saw confirmed the information we received. Neither in dress nor appearance were they distinguishable from ordinary labourers, except, perhaps, as having a somewhat more subdued and staid demeanour. The bailiff, who was superintending their work, told us that having had charge of gangs of labourers in many parts of Ireland, he had never found men more tractable or willing to work than these prisoners; adding, what would rarely be the case with free labourers, that an oath or indecent expression was unheard among them. This statement was confirmed by the other officers. It was difficult to conceive that these were men of the same class as those whose scowling or knavish visages we had seen in photograph or in flesh, in the first stage at Mountjoy; yet undoubtedly they had passed through that prison.

"A doubt having been suggested, by what we heard and saw of prisoners in the later stages of their imprisonment, and after discharge, as to whether they really were of the same criminal class as our English convicts, we examined such specimens of the *raw material*, so to speak, on which the Irish system has to work, as this prison presented. Photographs have been taken of the prisoners on their admission; and certainly, making every allowance for the well-known fact that the photograph does not flatter, a series of physiognomies expressing more unmitigated ruffianism than the volume of portraits which we saw presents, it were difficult to conceive. The living specimens, whom we visited in their cells, had no less the aspect of knavish cunning or sullen brutality, with which our experience at Wakefield has made us familiar. We saw men with whom a tête-à-tête interview produced a sensation decidedly disagreeable, and whose look afforded some excuse for the precaution, objectionable as it seemed to us, by which the warders are armed with truncheons, ' in case,' as was said, ' of an attack by a wicked prisoner.'

"The records of the offences for which the prisoners were convicted, also show that they are persons of much the same class as those with whom we have to deal in the English convict prisons, thieves and burglars forming a large majority.

"Our experience as regards the Irish prisoner in English prisons, has not led us to believe that he is of more amiable character, or easier to manage and reform, than his 'erring brother,' born on this side the Channel.

"The character of the Irish convicts previous to the introduction of the improved discipline, was so exceedingly bad, that a special request was sent from Western Australia, September, 1854, that no more of them might be sent to that colony, though it was willing to receive English convicts.

"After such testimony as to the past, and our own observations as to the present, when we find the remarkable extent to which it has been found practicable to carry the abandonment of 'coercion,' and the substitution of 'moral agencies,' in the later stages of the Irish convict discipline, and the satisfactory results which have followed, we feel bound to attribute those results to *good management*, and the excellence of the system, rather than to any antecedent superiority in the character of the Irish convict."

Lusk prison remains to the present time, ten years since the support and influence of the originator of the system has left it, a monument of the truth of his principles.

CHAPTER III.

THE system of liberating convicts on a conditional discharge was first introduced in the Penal Settlements of the British Colonies, where men who had been transported were, after a time, set at liberty under certain conditions. But a large number of men remained in confinement in England who had received sentences of transportation, about 9,000 at the end of 1852, when transportation was discontinued; the sentences were always long, as it was intended that they should be abridged nearly one-half by good conduct under confinement. The system of conditional freedom was therefore extended to them also. It appeared to possess great advantages, and to be founded on a true principle.

Since it is quite impossible that the reformation of any one can be relied on as real, as long as he is in an unnatural condition and under coercion, which he must be while in prison, to give a convict his freedom, under condition that it shall be forfeited at once if he proves by his conduct that he is not reformed, is evidently a most satisfactory way of ascertaining the safety to the public of his return to society. Besides, the slight controul and surveillance which are implied in the license itself, and essential to the development of the system, are an excellent preparation to one whose voluntary action has been cramped for many years, to enable him to use his liberty without abusing it.

The following conditions are indorsed on the license of every convict so liberated in the United Kingdom :—

" NOTICE.

"1. The power of revoking or altering the License of a Convict will most certainly be exercised in case of his misconduct.

" 2 If, therefore, he wishes to retain the privilege, which by his good behaviour under Penal Discipline he has obtained, he must prove by his subsequent conduct that he is really worthy of Her Majesty's clemency.

" 3. To produce a forfeiture of the License *it is by no means necessary that the holder should be convicted of any new offence. If he associates with notoriously bad characters, leads an idle and dissolute life, or has no visible means of obtaining an honest livelihood, &c., it will be assumed that he is about to relapse into crime, and he will be at once apprehended, and recommitted to prison under his original sentence."*

This notice is so explicit, and so distinctly asserts that a new offence is not necessary for the forfeiture of the license, that the public at first reposed confidence in the Government that its provisions would be carried into effect. But it soon became evident that in England no means were being taken to enforce the conditions of the license, that the whole of the warning to the convict was a mere delusion, that this ticket-of-leave was quite unnecessary to protect the convict from the danger of being apprehended as a runaway from prison, and did not defend the public from the risk of being at the mercy of unreformed criminals. This official document was, then, a mere useless form, which the convict, for his own safety, would generally hasten to destroy, as being a silent witness against him in any new crime he may commit.

It was evident that something was deficient in the working of a system which, in principle, appeared so excellent. The subject was brought before Parliament, and in 1856 a Select Committee of the House of Commons was appointed to consider the whole subject. It thus appeared, from the evidence of many official witnesses, that the convicts who obtained licenses for conditional discharge were not really reformed; that no supervision was exercised over them when at liberty, but that on the contrary the London police had especial orders not to interfere with them; that when license holders were known to be living disorderly lives, they were not interfered with, and that some legal difficulty appeared to exist to the revocation of a ticket-of-leave, except on their being convicted of an absolute crime. It was also believed that the supervision of convicts by the police would be likely to prevent the convict when at large from obtaining work, and it was therefore discouraged. The public, therefore, had a profound distrust of a ticket-of-leave man. It appeared, however, from the evidence brought before the Committee, that though the most serious evils had arisen from the manner in which the system had been worked, yet that the principle was in itself sound, and might with other arrangements be developed in the manner originally intended.

The following conditions must exist, to secure the successful working of the Ticket-of-leave System, and the consequent absorbtion of the convict into society.

First,—The penal system must be such as to inspire general confidence that it is likely to produce a reformatory effect on the persons subjected to it.

Secondly,—Before release, the prisoner should be placed in such a condition of comparative liberty, and should have such degree of exercise of his own will, as may enable him to give some reliable proof of his determination henceforth to choose good and to eschew evil.

Thirdly,—He should be for some time after his discharge in a state of *conditional* liberty, so that, if he proves by his conduct that he is not reformed, and and is likely again to injure society, he may be sent back to a longer period of discipline.

Fourthly,—There should be such a system of supervision over the convict during his state of conditional liberty, as should aid him rather than hinder him in his honest endeavours to do right, while it should inspire in his mind a certainty that return to incarceration would be the certain consequence of his infringement of the conditions on which he was liberated.

We have already seen how the Irish Convict Prisons under the management of Sir Walter Crofton and his Co-Directors fulfilled the two first of these conditions. The development of this last stage, the conditional liberation of the convict, leading finally to his absorbtion into society, is the subject of this chapter.

The Directors of the Irish Convict Prisons were so sensible of the danger of releasing prisoners before they had proved themselves fit for freedom, that they did not venture for the first two years of their management to issue any ticket-of-leave, and it was only after their experiment of the Intermediate Prisons that this was attempted. About seventy-five per cent. passed through that stage and obtained a license. The remaining twenty-five were discharged direct from the ordinary prisons—misconduct and offences having precluded their removal. We now speak only of the former portion. Some of these, having saved sufficient money to pay their passage to a distant country where there was a greater demand for labour, emigrated as soon as they were at liberty. The remainder were the subject of the system of supervision adopted.

The following memorandum, issued under the sanction of the late Earl of Carlisle, then Viceroy of Ireland, shows the system adopted :—

" MEMORANDUM. " DUBLIN CASTLE, 1st *January*, 1857.

" REGISTRATION AND SUPERVISION OF CONVICTS ON TICKET OF LICENSE.

" His Excellency the Lord Lieutenant being desirous of accurately testing the practical working of the Ticket of License System, by a well-organized system of registration of licensed convicts, whereby they may be brought under special supervision, and a check be laid upon the evil disposed, has been pleased to sanction the following regulations, which are, therefore, circulated for the information and guidance of the constabulary.

" 1. When an offer of employment for a prisoner is accepted, a notification thereof will be made by the Directors of Government Prisons to the Inspector-General of Constabulary, by whom it will be transmitted to the constabulary of the locality in which the employment is to be given, with all necessary particulars for the purpose of being entered in a register at the Constabulary Station.

" 2. Each convict so to be employed will report himself at the appointed Constabulary Station (the name of which will be given to him) on his arrival in the district, and, subsequently, on the 1st of each month.

" 3. A special report is to be made to Head Quarters by the constabulary whenever they shall observe a convict on license guilty of misconduct or leading an irregular life.

" 4. A convict is not to change his locality without notifying the circumstances at the Constabulary Station, in order that his registration may be transferred to the place to which he is about to proceed. On his arrival he must report himself to the nearest Constabulary Station (of the name of which he is to be informed), and such transfer is to be reported to Head Quarters for the information of the Directors of Government Prisons.

" 5. An infringement of these rules by the convict will cause it to be assumed that he is leading an idle, irregular life, and therefore entail the revocation of his license.

" 6. Further regulations may hereafter be added to the foregoing should they become necessary.

" It will be obvious that as the employer is in every case
made acquainted with the antecedents of the prisoner he wishes
to engage, any inquiries that may afterwards be discreetly made,
as to character, conduct, &c., cannot in any way affect the prospects of the convict. The managers of the refuges for female
prisoners favourably account for ninety-six out of ninety-seven
female convicts up to the 31st of August, 1857 (the license of
one has been revoked). It appears that on the whole number
of 559 convicts on license up to the 30th September, 1857,
seventeen licenses have been revoked. It will be observed also
that in addition to the stringent observation exercised over
forty-two men who are, many of them, exposed to the temptations
of the city of Dublin, there is also the very efficient and general
supervision of the constabulary. Yet the results, though slight
irregularities are always noted, and the terms of the license
most strictly enforced,* prove the revocation of rather more
than three per cent."

The obtaining work for the licensed convicts,
before the system which has been adopted was
generally understood was at first a matter of some
difficulty. The Directors were fortunate in having
the services of the late Mr. Organ, who, as lecturer
in the prison, nobly devoted himself to the work.
He gives the following account of it in his evidence
before the Royal Commission in 1863 :—

" At the outset it was a labour of great difficulty
to procure employment for those men on their dis-

---

* As corroboration of the practice pursued, I may add that two of these
revocations of license have been on account of irregularity in reporting
themselves ; three for keeping bad company ; one for losing his employment through drink ; one for fighting and brawling in the streets ; one for
defrauding the railway company by travelling without taking a ticket.

charge. I commenced my duties in February, 1856.
I drew out a map of the county of Dublin, dividing
it into baronies, laying down upon this map the
different post towns, also the mills, and factories, and
farms, showing the names of the proprietors, the
nature of those works, and so on. Having done
this, I set out to see such and such employer. Sometimes I was scoffed at, and on more than one occasion
the hall door was closed in my face. Still I perse-
vered, and I was very well satisfied, if, after going a
distance of 40 or 50 miles, I should meet with one
employer who would give one of my Smithfield men
a chance to work out his character once more. When
I secured one, I visited both the employer and the
employed, and I continue to do so down to the present
time. The employer would ask me what controul I
had, or the Government had, over the men. I, of
course, explained, but I will give a case in point.
Some five years ago I went to a gentleman who was
a very large employer, and I saw him. I explained
to him my mission. I was a long time in inducing him
to give me ɩ chance, but after many repeated visits I
did succeed. He took one man. I visited that man
once a fortnight, although he had removed from
Dublin a distance of ten miles, and I visited the
employer. That man succeeded in giving the employer
satisfaction, and the employer afterwards applied for
another, afterwards for another, and previous to my
leaving Dublin this employer wrote the following
letter, dated 21st February, 1863 :—' Dear Sir,—In

reply to your letter, I beg leave to state that it was at your earnest solicitation that I was induced to take convicts into my employment, in the first instance. I have now had fully five years' experience of them, during which time they have given me universal satisfaction. I have one at present in my employment, in whose honesty I have such confidence that I have made him a sort of watchman, and he has for the last few days detected parties robbing me. Another saved enough to enable him to emigrate to Australia. A third, in shovelling up some manure, found a silver spoon, which he at once gave me. In conclusion I can only say that whenever you have an able-bodied man whom you can recommend, it will afford me much pleasure to give him employment.' This employer was one whom I secured, I assure you, after a great deal of trouble, through the character and conduct of the first man he had employed. I found great difficulty at first in procuring employment for them, but that difficulty has diminished since the employers have had experience of the men. Since such employers as these have been found, the difficulty, of course, does not exist now to so great an extent; but I think that, if I were to go over the same task again with other employers, I should have the same difficulty to encounter.

" My bi-monthly visits are valued very much by employers, who frequently say to me, ' I do not like to speak to the man for doing so and so. You had

better do so ; he will attend more to what you say
than what I say.' I have frequently, in a country
place, got 9 or 10 of these men behind a hayrick,
and advised them what to do ; in many cases they
take a greater interest in their employment than
ordinary workmen do, because they know that the
employers have taken them out of prison, and thrown,
as it were, a cloak of protection over them. * * *

"Referring to the connection between the police
and myself, when I find that a man is not going on
according to my liking, and he has something suspicious about him, I go to the Director, and I either
bring the man up if within reach, or tell him about
it. I say, 'I do not like the way in which this man
is going on ;' he may have too smooth an appearance
for a hard-working man, or he may be lounging
about, or I might find him in his home when he
should be out working, or out when he should be in ;
then the director takes a note of that ; at the same
time, if it happens that my suspicions are aroused at
night, or when the Director is not in the office, and
the case is an urgent one, I do not wait for the
director to come the following morning, but I go
straight to the detective office at the castle-yard ; I
there tell the officiating inspector my doubts, and he,
as a matter of course, has a close eye upon that man.
Then in cases of suspicion I inform the detective
authorities ; they know that it is their interest and
my interest to work hand-in-hand ; and I point out
to them sometimes, when I have my documents con-

venient, the last observation I have made upon the man. * * *

"I explain to the persons who employ these men, the controul which the Government has over them whilst they are holders of a ticket-of-leave. I always lay the facts clearly before the employers, because if I were not straightforward with them, and I was once detected, I should never be able to show my face again. So that the employers are aware that these men whom they take into their service have been previously in the Convict Prisons. But the men with whom they work are not always aware of that fact. It is the interest of the employers to keep the other workmen in ignorance of the fact; and there is another thing, that if the honest workmen were to know this, I am sure they would take objection to it, and make the place too hot for a discharged prisoner. No difficulty has been found in keeping the matter concealed from the other workmen. The employer always does so. He communicates with me privately, and the other workmen are not acquainted with the characters of the men or their previous mode of life.

"I do not find any indisposition on their part to continue this intercourse with me, which they were obliged to keep up while under their tickets-of-leave ; on the contrary, they appear to be grateful for what I have done for them. The success of the system very greatly depends upon its being possible to prevent the men who have been discharged from being recognised as former convicts, but in every case to let the employer know all about them. * * *

"I have known cases in which the old associates of convicts have endeavoured to use their power over them, and from a fear of being betrayed to extort money from them. I have seen their former companions waiting in knots on the morning of their discharge, and endeavouring to induce them to go with them. I have known their former associates to come up 100 miles from different parts of Ireland in order to meet them on the morning of their discharge, and induce them to follow them. When men are on the point of leaving me, I impress upon them to the greatest possible degree the danger that will arise to them, and which they will have to meet amongst their old companions; because, if a well-disposed convict on being discharged is anxious to earn his bread honestly, and goes in amongst his former companions he is sneered at and he is tormented, in fact he has not any power to resist. I have known also in my tours amongst these people, where there has been a badly-disposed convict, much harm to be done. Whatever improvement might be made in the system of prison discipline, it would still remain very desirable that convicts, after their discharge, should go to some new place where it would be more easy for them to pursue an honest course of life, for I think that the advantages to a man in a new place would be more numerous; at the same time I would not have convicts after their discharge when they were free in the world link themselves with one another, or associate together. I would prefer to separate them and scatter them as much as possible.

" In case a license holder changes his place of residence without reporting himself, I consider that that is a breach of the conditions of the license ; he may be robbing. In such a case, the Director would notify the case to the police. I believe that he gives a certain time for a man to turn up, say a fortnight or so, and if he does not turn up he is then put in the ' Hue and Cry,' and his license is revoked, for leaving his place of residence without notifying it in the proper manner. The license is always revoked in the case of a man who leaves his place of residence without notifying it to the proper authorities. If they go away from their residences without giving notice, so that we cannot find them out, their names are handed over to the police, and they are put into the ' Hue and Cry ;' their license certainly is revoked. Suppose a man remains in his residence in Dublin, but we are aware he is associating with bad characters and frequenting public-houses, that man's license would be revoked."

In Dublin there is a fortnightly visitation of the convicts by Mr. Organ, and a return made of their employment, conduct, &c. Inquirers from England, Scotland and the Continent, have repeatedly tested this fact ; and have afterwards satisfied themselves that the antecedents of those visited by them have been " habitually criminal."

The nature of this supervision is so unique, as well as successful, and has not only been the subject of so much discussion, but has excited so much cavil

and scepticism, that it will be well to take Sir W.
Crofton's own official account of it, as given to the
Royal Commissioners, in reply to their very close
examination ; — it will thus appear how official
arrangements supported voluntary effort.

" The Dublin supervision commenced in the year
before the supervision of the constabulary, viz., in
January, 1856 ; the supervision in the country began
in January, 1857. The plan of the Dublin supervision was, that the lecturer should visit every man
who was out on ticket-of-leave officially, and bring
in a fortnightly return to my office, and go into each
case with me, and show in the return the employer's
name, the standard of wages, and the conduct of the
men ; this fortnightly return was filed in the office
afterwards. I always had this information checked,
when necessary, by a detective inspector of police. I
used to call him in in every case that presented difficulty. If Mr. Organ found in his visits that there was
any obstruction to his obtaining from the convict full
information, he was at once handed over to the
observation of the police, in order that they might
see very closely whether there was any chance of his
infringing his license.

" Mr. Organ saw these men individually every
fortnight, and reported on them to me, with the
names of their employers. This detective inspector
attended at my office two or three times a week, and
when he had any notice of failures, as he had sometimes, he used to tell me of them ; he consulted with

me, and then made a return immediately of the exact state of the case. Wo had thus a direct police check upon Mr. Organ's reports. Finding in 1856 that some of the men might go into the country from Dublin and defeat us altogether, wo were led at once to the necessity of having police supervision in the country. We were in a very false position as to the public in general, from not being able to account for the ticket-of-leave convicts. Wo felt that we must be able to say where these men were, or it would produce such a panic that the men would never get employment at all. With regard to the supervision in Dublin, nothing can be more strict, for when anything bad is heard about a man his license is revoked immediately, and there is this fortnightly official list kept as a check. This is merely a portion or extract from the list *(the same being handed in)*; extracts from Mr. Organ's usual fortnightly reports; he has not confined himself simply to the prisoners discharged on ticket-of-leave, but he has habitually visited, also, other men who have been discharged under the Penal Servitude Act of 1853, whose sentences had expired, but who still reside in Dublin. over whom we have no legal check, but obtain this information. He has visited them and placed them on our reports as well as the others; it is of course clear that any of these men unconditionally discharged could have closed their doors against him if they had wished, but this visitation has extended over some 400 or 500 people of this class in Dublin. It is of importance because it brings a certain knowledge of these people to us that could not be attained in any other way, both as to the result of our system and the lives they were leading. This report refers to what are called the old Act men—that means men who had been under sentence of transportation, and this document is with reference to men who were under sentence of transportation. The first case that I come to is that of a man whose crime was burglary, there were former convictions, he had been bad in crime for eight years; there is his name, his residence, his employer's name, and his employment, and his wages. The date of his conviction was in 1852, and he was discharged from the Convict Prisons the 9th September, 1857, he is still reported upon; he commenced to work at 8s. a week, but now his wages are much higher. He had been sentenced to ten years' transportation; he was convicted in 1852 and his term expired in 1862, he is still on the list. In the next case the crime was burglary, former convictions, and for years in crime; he was employed under a public body, his name is given, his residence, and wages; he has been out since the 5th of July, 1857. That was a case of ten years' transportation. It also gives the general conduct of those men; there are observations to every one of them. I think that there are something like 140 men under the supervision of Mr. Organ, in Dublin, at this moment.

"I had, when in office, constant communication with the detective officers in the Dublin police, who were assisting Mr. Organ in the supervision of these men. They were a very material assistance to me in carrying out the supervision. They took a considerable amount of trouble when a case required it.

".Mr. Organ always went to the house of the employer and saw the man and the employer. The man was sent for and Mr. Organ then spoke to him.

" I never heard that the circumstance of his going to visit these men so frequently was a means of discovering to their fellow workmen who they were. The employers themselves, so far from objecting to his visits, encouraged them, and considered them to a very great extent a protection to themselves.

" The slightest infringement of the conditions of the license leads to a revocation of it. *I do not believe—and I have often put this forth when I was in the department—that any case could be proved of a man breaking the conditions of his license in Ireland, and remaining at large; he was sure to be put back to separation, and his license revoked.*

" If we found that a man was within a fortnight of the expiration of his sentence, and had infringed some of the conditions of the ticket-of-leave, we sent that man back to prison, for the sake of the principle. I do not know that it has ever occurred in a case so close as a fortnight, but it has done so close as a month or three weeks. The circumstance of his sentence being so nearly expired did not interfere with that in the slightest degree.

"They were generally easily caught. They were put in the 'Hue and Cry,' a warrant was issued, and there were very few cases in which they baffled us. At first there were a great many shifts and trials to evade, but ultimately and before long, when they found that many had their licenses revoked, and were brought back, they did not even try to baffle us as they did at first.

"In the county prisons, when prisoners are suspected or known to have been convicts, they send up a form containing particulars, with a description of the person suspected or known to be a discharged convict. That comes to the convict prison office, in order that the man may be identified ; and very often when it is necessary, if a man at all demurs to his identification, a prison officer is sent down to identify him, and if found guilty of any crime, a letter is in all cases placed on the table of the judicial officer, which has been written to the governor of the gaol, the letter being in these terms : — 'Government Prisons' Office.—Sir,—The enclosed particulars of —————— ———— have been compared with the books of this office, and are correct. In the event of his being found guilty of the present charge the directors of convict prisons request that the notice of the judge may be particularly called to the circumstance of his being an 'habitual offender,' with the view of his receiving a sentence proportionate to his perseverance in pursuing a course of crime. Please to notify the result of the trial to this office, and return the enclosure at the same time.' This is a case which actually occurred. A man was convicted for picking pockets. He was a convict, and this course was pursued with him. It entailed upon him a sentence of ten years' penal servitude. His character as an habitual criminal was taken into consideration by the judge. I am able to speak confidently on two most important points—information with regard to habitual offenders being sent in each case to the county prisons; and in the case of ticket-of-leave men that their licenses have been always revoked for an infringement of the conditions.

" It is not very difficult for an officer in Dublin to recognise a man of whom a description is sent from a provincial town. He has had this man perhaps within the last four or five years in his custody, and besides the general description, and the aid of photography, there is a margin left for observations; practically it is found that very few come into the Convict Prisons who have not been known in some way, and whose identification has not been made. The result is that the practice succeeds in a very great majority of cases, and operates very beneficially upon the minds of the convicts.

" The supervision of convicts in the country is thus carried on by the constabulary. There is a notification made to the inspector-general of the constabulary the moment a man is liberated, stating to what district he is going; the man then registers himself with the head of the police, states what he

is going to do, where he is going to be employed,
and reports himself to him once a month. If he
removes from that district, his registration is transferred from the district he is in at that time, to the
one to which he goes, so that he is traced from one
place to another. If he does anything to infringe
the terms of his license, the constabulary report him,
and his license is revoked at once.

" He must come himself once a month, and
report himself to the police, but it is evident that the
police do not confine themselves to that, for, knowing
where he is, they would look after him a little oftener,
without interfering with him. I can state from my
own experience that there is no undue espionage or
oppression practised by the police.

" In the first instance I had a very large number
of complaints from the convicts generally ; they came
almost in a body, stating that they would rather be
kept to the end of their sentences than go out with such
a stigma ; but as it was quite evident that they would
have had to remain to the end of their sentences, as
they could not get out on any other terms, that feeling very shortly vanished, and they preferred being
placed under police supervision. I have seen some
hundreds of these people after being subjected to
supervision, and with the exception of two cases, in
which I recollect complaints being made of interference, nothing detrimental occurred. I state
distinctly that in my opinion there has been no undue
interference on the part of the police. It is quite

probable that some man, when doing wrong, would state that he had been interfered with; but I know in general practice it is not true.

" I am quite sure that if police supervision were withdrawn to-morrow from the licensed convicts in Ireland, you would find but little employment for them, and you would have very serious trouble. I have no doubt that it is a very great protection to the public in Ireland."

The foregoing account of the manner in which the Ticket-of-leave System with the supervision of licensed convicts was developed in connection with the Irish Convict Prisons, demonstrates that the principle on which it was founded was sound, and its application to ordinary circumstances very possible, provided the essential conditions are complied with.

These conditions are:—

First,—That the prison system shall have been of such a nature as to afford a reasonable expectation that convicts who have obtained a license are prepared for liberty.

Secondly,—That the terms of the license are strictly observed.

Thirdly,—That there are such police arrangements in the country, and such registration of convicts as will ensure *certainty* both in the minds of the convicts and of the public that all violation of the conditions of the license will involve return to punishment.

Fourthly, — That voluntary benevolent effort, acting in concert with police regulation, shall coöpe-

F

rate with the convict in obtaining his readmission to society.

The late Mr. Organ admirably fulfilled the last condition; his devoted zeal and loving perseverance produced effects which will rarely be equalled. But the same work may be carried on by societies in aid, if wisely managed and benevolently carried out. The system is well known on the Continent. In the Appendix to the Committee on Transportation in 1856 appears a *resumé* of replies to inquiries made by our Government to many Courts of Europe, respecting the system adopted by them in the disposal of criminals. From this it appears that in most states a degree of police supervision is exercised for a long time after the release of a criminal, and that in some a number of years of supervision is made part of the sentence. Care is at the same time taken on the liberation of a convict to afford him every facility for obtaining honest employment. Private societies are also very generally instituted to coöperate with the Government in the restoration of the offender, and in some cases the supervison is intrusted to them.

It is by such coöperation only, between the Government and voluntary benevolent effort, that any prison system can be rendered effective to diminish the crime of a country, or at least to prevent its increase.

CHAPTER IV.

ALL who have had any practical acquaintance with the management of convicted women, are fully aware that it is one of the most difficult problems to be satisfactorily solved.

The organization of women, both mental and physical, is much more delicate and sensitive than that of men, and also is subject to peculiar conditions;—it follows from this that when morally diseased and in an abnormal state, their reformation, and restoration to a healthy condition, is far more difficult than that of the other sex. The structure of society, besides, precludes the adoption of such a system for women as has been found to work admirably for men. This is well known to all who have undertaken the care of females, young or old, and in whatever condition of life, who are mentally, morally, or physically diseased.

The evidence submitted to the Royal Commission on Prison Discipline in 1863, by the Directors of the English Convict Prisons, and other official gentlemen, painfully confirm these statements. The Director of the Female Prisons, frankly avowed his inability to check the evils existing in them, which had been made known to the public by some volumes which excited at the time considerable notice.

The women of this degraded portion of society will be generally found to differ in many respects from those belonging to a higher sphere. Their intellectual powers are low, and from having been left uncultivated, are in a state of torpidity from which it is very difficult to rouse them. This peculiarly low intellectual condition in females of the lowest social grade is accompanied by a very strong development of the passions and of the lower nature. Extreme excitability, violent and even frantic outbursts of passion, a duplicity and disregard of truth hardly conceivable in the better classes of society, render all attempts to improve them peculiarly difficult. And if, added to all this, what is holiest and best in woman has been perverted and diseased by unlawful intercourse with the other sex, as is very frequently the case, there is engendered in her a hardness of heart, a corruption of the whole nature, which would seem to make absolute reformation almost impossible. We have heard one who had had large experience in the temperance cause declare that he never yet had known a reformed female drunkard, though he could point to multitudes of men who had been rescued from the sway of intoxicating liquors. Most seldom is any real change observable in a woman who has arrived at maturity in so degraded a condition.

In order to have any prospect of success in the reformation of women in this very degraded and, we may say, abnormal condition, for their characteristics differ essentially from those of the labouring, middle and upper classes, there must exist, in the first place, firm steady controul, against which it is evidently hopeless to rebel, combined with a strict and vigilant discipline, administered with the most impartial justice. In the next place, to provide abundance of active useful work is absolutely necessary. The restless excitable nature of these women requires a vent in something; they should have full employment, of a kind which will exercise their muscles and fully occupy their minds, so as to calm their spirits and satisfy them with the feeling of having accomplished something. These two primary conditions having been arranged satisfactorily, considerable attention must at the same time be paid to the culture of the intellectual powers. These, we have already stated, are more deadened, or perverted to a bad use in women than in men. There is far greater difficulty in stimulating to mental exertion girls who have passed their childhood in neglect, than boys. The effort of learning to read is to such often positively painful, and without the greatest skill, kindness, and firmness combined on the part of the teacher, the young person succumbs to the difficulty. The effort once made and a triumph achieved, an important step in reformation is attained, for stores of interesting information are now open which will fill the mind,

instead of the pernicious thoughts which formerly
harboured there. Intellectual effort, which would be
very easy and pleasant to a child of six years old, is
extremely difficult and unpleasant to a girl of sixteen,
still more so to a woman of thirty or upwards;—a
mastery over it once gained, not only an intellectual
but a moral power is acquired, both of which facilitate the work of reformation. Another essential part
of the work of reforming such women as have been
described, is the healthy development of their affections. These are peculiarly strong in the female sex,
and may be made the means of calling out the highest
virtues, the most genuine self-devotion; when perverted, they may be, and are frequently, made an
instrument of much evil; but in a woman they can
never be utterly lost. It will then be essential to the
success of any system which has as its object the
reformation of women, that scope should be given to
the affectional part of the woman's nature, and that
this should be enlisted on the side of virtue.

That all these conditions should be fulfilled in a
Convict Prison does certainly appear very difficult;
yet, if they are essential to success, no labour, no
expense, should be deemed too great to develop a
system which should embody them all, and do the
work required,—reform female convicts. The expense
which a bad woman is to the public, who comes forth
from a lengthened confinement in a Government gaol
unreformed, is far greater than any possible cost
which might have been incurred in reforming her;

the evil she has done within the prison to those around her is very great, and extends the poisonous influence to a widely-extending circle, when the women she has corrupted go out into the world; on her own discharge she emerges from her seclusion only to plunge into greater excesses than before, and to perpetuate and intensify the pollution of the moral atmosphere from which she had been temporarily withdrawn.

Keeping in view the foregoing remarks, we shall now proceed to give an account of the system successfully pursued in the Irish Female Convict Prisons, under the direction of Sir Walter Crofton.

The condition of the Female Convict Prisons in Ireland was even worse than that of those for males, when the Directors first undertook the charge. The female convicts who had been transported to Western Australia had been so bad that the colony absolutely refused to receive any others. The Directors say in their first report :—

" Our proportion of female criminals is very large, and it is much to be deplored that such is the case, considering the influence for good or evil that women must exercise on the rising generation. This large proportion may, in a great measure, be ascribed to the circumstances of the country, and want of industrial employment. A prison is now erecting at Mountjoy for the reception of 600 female convicts; which will, we trust, enable us, from its construction, to carry out such penal and reformatory treatment as will induce habits of reflection and amendment, and will also relieve the County Gaols from the great inconvenience to which they are subjected through the reception of Government prisoners. Pending its erection, however, we are endeavouring to ameliorate, if possible, the condition of those confined in Grange-gorman and Cork Prisons, which, unfortunately, can only hold a portion of our convicts. Towards attaining this object, education adapted to the wants of that class, and engendering habits of industry, are the great adjuncts to the religious influence inculcated by their chaplains. With regard to education, the Female Prison Schools, in common with the others, will be placed under the inspection of the National Board of Education. Heretofore instruction has been limited to those under twenty-seven or twenty-eight years : we have given directions that there should be no limit as to age provided there is a disposition to acquire information.

" Respecting industrial training, we have desired that all the convicts should, in turn, receive instruction in cooking, laundry, sewing, knitting, cleaning, &c., instead of confining a certain number to a particular occupation; although this plan tends to the work not being so well performed, we prefer it on account of the advantages gained by the individuals receiving general instruction.

" It has been a custom to admit convicts into the prison with their children sometimes at the age of five or six years; we cannot consider such places, with their necessary associations, advantageous for education of the young, and recommend its discontinuance, excepting in cases of children under two years of age."

In their second report they show that immediate good results have followed the adoption of their plans. They say:—

" With regard to female convicts, we have devoted much attention to carry out the plans proposed in our last year's report concerning them, and have observed a manifest improvement in their general demeanour and conduct. This we attribute in some measure to the efforts made by our teachers to open their minds by education, and to engender habits of self-controul. Many, instead of sullenly brooding over their past life, now look forward with hope to the future. Even women advanced in life, who have spent most of their career in prison, and who at first would not attend school, and seemed incapable of understanding the advantages of education, are now amongst the most assiduous in their classes. A difference in their conduct is already apparent; they are more orderly and obedient to the rules, and make efforts to exercise that self-command, the want of which has so often led them into crime. We trust that under the new arrangements in the prisons, and a system of refuges and patronage on discharge, which we are now advocating, many convicts formerly considered irreclaimable, will finish their career as good members of society.

"On the subject of education, Mrs. Lidwell, the Superintendent of the Cork Depôt, expresses herself as follows:—'I find that the effect of school instruction has been, in most instances, to awaken, as it were, the minds of the prisoners, and improve their natural comprehensions, to make them more docile, more easily brought to see the value of cleanliness and order, and to inspire them with a considerable feeling of self-respect ; many of them seem by education to have become better able to understand the folly and wickedness of their previous lives, and experience a strong feeling of repentance. I have observed, too, that as they make progress in school education, their conduct in the prison proportionally improves ; and that some who have come from the County Gaols with very turbulent characters, and apparently of very violent dispositions, become, under the influence of education, conformable to discipline.' "

The minds of the Directors were awakened to the importance of devising some plan for the gradual introduction to liberty of the female convicts, while at the same time they should be brought into personal contact of ladies unconnected with the prisons, who would devote to them their voluntary benevolent effort. They continue :—

"Great difficulties present themselves in the final disposal of female convicts. A man can obtain employment in various ways in out-door service, not requiring, in all cases, special reference to character, and at work which is not open to females in this.

country. A woman, immediately on discharge from
prison, is totally deprived of any honest means of
obtaining a livelihood. Persons of her own class
will object to associate in labour with her, even if
employers were willing to give her work; and the
well-conducted portion of the community object to
receive with their families, or domestic servants,
persons so circumstanced, without a stronger guarantee and proof of their real and permanent reformation, than would be afforded by a prison character."

How to effect this was the grand problem to be
solved. The difficulty is thus concisely set forth by
the Directors:—"A Government Institution would
answer for a mere refuge, *but not as a medium through
which the individual will be established in society ;* for
under any rules it will be looked upon as a prison,
and on the discharge of the inmates the same difficulties will be felt as at present in our Convict
Depôts."

To give such confidence to the public in the reformation of these unhappy women, as to make families
willing to receive them into their domestic circle, it
was necessary that the female convicts should not
only have gone through some such intermediate stage
as the men, but that they should have had some kind
of trial of the sincerity of their reformation without
the restraint of the prison walls, or the guardianship
of government officials. The plan proposed by the
Directors admirably combined these objects. "For
this reason," they continue, "instead of increasing

the existing Government Prison Establishments—a plan attended with much expense, delay, and difficulty—we proposed, in December last, to the Irish Government, that convicts whose conduct had been exemplary should be drafted into existing private charitable institutions willing to receive them, where the disposition of each inmate would be studied, and the certificate of character founded on that study, together with recommendations, which would then be considered sufficiently satisfactory to obtain her employment; the prisoners, in all such institutions, should be under the general supervision and inspection of the Convict Directors. In order to carry out this plan, a certain number of exemplary convicts should be selected from the Government Prisons, at periods varying according to circumstances, previous to the time when in the usual course they would become eligible for discharge, and be sent to such private establishments, and not released therefrom under at least three months; and not then unless immediate and proper employment should offer, excepting, however, cases where prisoners become regularly entitled to their discharges, from having completed their sentence, and special cases to be determined on by the Directors and sanctioned by the Executive. Should, however, a prisoner misconduct herself, she would be liable to recommittal to the Convict Depôt, to undergo her original sentence. It is obviously most desirable to enlist public sympathy and interest in any scheme for the employment of discharged female prisoner*; this object we consider will bo best attained in tho manner proposed."

Here wo have tho first sketch of a plan which has succeeded admirably.

Two Refuges wore at once established. One was a largo convent of tho Sisters of Mercy at Golden Bridge, near Dublin, tho other was a Protestant refuge in Heytesbury Street, established purposely by some benevolent ladies.

It required some moral courage, or rather a strong faith and a devoted love in those ladies, unaided by means of punishment, or of physical restraint, to undertake the custody and care of women who had sprung from " a class so depraved, and hitherto deemed so incorrigible," continues tho Report, " as to bo absolutely rejected by tho colonists of Western Australia, a colony whose vitality at tho present moment depends on an increase of tho female sex."

These Refuges form a valuable link to society, or they aro accessible to the public, whoso cöoperation is so important. Many visitors from England who, in 1861, attended tho Social Scionco Association in Dublin, closely inspected them, and received every desired information as to their working. All were struck with the changed look and manner of the women from what had been noticed in tho earlier stages. There was nothing to remind ono that they had even been in prison; and they were ready to converse with visitors with full assurance of sympathy respecting their future prospects. In the autumn of the same year, the four Yorkshire Magistrates who went over, closely scrutinized this important part of the Irish Convict System. In their published "Observations" they say:—

"We visited two refuges in Dublin—a larger one for Roman Catholic women, who are the most numerous, at Golden Bridge; and a smaller one for Protestants in Heytesbury Street. The former is conducted by Sisters of Mercy, some of whom were ladies of high social position. * * * The women are generally found exhibiting the most willing obedience to discipline, and among them misconduct of any kind is extremely rare. Considering that many of them are women who have been convicted over and over again, the fact speaks volumes for the salutary effect of the training they have previously undergone in prison. No difficulty was said to be found in procuring situations for them, which shows how well the refuge answers the purpose for which it was intended. The Protestant Refuge is under the charge of a Matron, superintended by a committee of lady visitors. We were much struck by the apparent industry displayed in the washhouse and laundry. * * * That, under these circumstances, women—and those women convicts—should be found to work as hard for the benefit of the institution where they are detained, as they would for themselves out of doors, appears to us a result of very high import, in a moral as well as in a financial point of view. It shows that an influence *yet unknown on this side the channel* has been brought to bear on the correction of that fault which is the special characteristic of the criminal class, viz., dislike of hard work."

To this may be added the personal testimony of the writer, as given in "Once a Week," June 7, 1862.

"IRISH CONVICT SYSTEM.—FEMALE PRISONS.

"No. IV.

"It is always a painful sight to see degraded women; but, on our recent visit to Dublin, we determined at once to encounter it, and our first visit in the capital of our Sister Isle was to the Mountjoy Female Convict Prison.

"It was the Sabbath, and it was an appropriate employment of the day consecrated to Him who came to seek and to save the lost, to worship with the prisoners. There are three distinct places of worship in Mountjoy Prison. The largest is for the Roman Catholics, adapted to the performance of the rites of their religion. A very plain, simple apartment is occupied by those attending the ministry of the Presbyterians, and a large chapel is simply arranged for worship, conducted according to the custom of the Church of England.

"In many prisons the convicts are arranged at public worship each in a separate cell or partition,

so as to see and be seen by the minister only,—as if
even in the presence of our Heavenly Father, and
engaged in His worship, the prison idea must still
pervade the service, and everything social be
banished. In other gaols, where there is not this
separation, but all worship God together, as an
absolute separation between the two sexes is necessary, the women are out of sight in a gallery. Here,
however, the women were alone in the chapel with the
clergyman and female officers, without any apparent
formality or restraint. A painful history might be
read on many of the countenances before us;—vice
dreadfully disfigures the features of a woman, and
no one could have been here without having gone
through a long course of crime. But all were join-
ing with apparent devotion and interest, every one
who could do so following the service in the prayer-
books; the earnest practical exhortations, which
were addressed to them in the sermon, were received apparently with self-application and intelligent
interest.

"The service concluded, the Lady-Superinten-
dent of the whole prison (who had not been present,
being a Roman Catholic), showed us the general
arrangements of the establishment, though of course
we were obliged to defer our observation of the
ordinary working of it to a week day. One feature
of it struck us particularly. In England the difficulties seem insuperable to the admission into gaols,
workhouses, and even infirmaries, of benevolent

lady visitors of different religious denominations.
In Ireland, where parties run high, we anticipated
still greater difficulties; yet here—in this Convict
Prison—the grand problem is solved, for not only
are the female officers of different religious denominations all working harmoniously together—but
Catholic, Church of England, and Presbyterian
ladies all visit the prisoners, with excellent effect,
and no interference with each other interrupts the
harmony of the establishment. All there are
engaged in one great work, and sympathise with
each other in it; judicious regulations being laid
down, which no one attempts to interfere with.
Each prisoner on entrance states her religious pro-
fession, and is expected to keep to it; and the ladies
of each denomination visit only those of the same
religion; they meet them in class, and, as occasion
presents itself, gain such knowledge of them as
enables the visitors to lend a helping hand to the
women when discharged. A good influence is thus
obtained: there is no proselytism; the motives of
the ladies cannot be questioned by the prisoners—
they come only to fulfil Christian duty; and these
wretched women, who are cut off from society
through their own crimes, here can feel that there are
those who care for their souls, and who are desirous
of giving them Christian sympathy. None but those
who personally know it, can comprehend the deep
import of the words, ' I was in prison and ye
visited me.'

" We had been told to be sure to see the Infant
School in the gaol! We were startled and shocked
at the bare idea. Are there even infants round
whom the prison walls are closed? Had not our
Reformatory and Industrial Schools been successful
in preserving young children from such an unnatural
condition? And then we remembered a dreadful
sight which we had once witnessed. In an Associated Gaol, we had been taken to a large room
appropriated to nursing mothers with their infants!
The room was full, and the spectacle awful! The
faces of those mothers can never be forgotten, for
they exhibited every species of hideous vice and
degradation. And these were to give the first
impressions to the young immortal beings who were
unhappily their children, and who were imbibing
from them the tainted streams of life. And not
only from its own mother would each child derive
its early impressions,—her face might perchance be
softened by a smile of maternal love,—but all around
there were other wicked mothers, whose looks and
voices would be bad and even fiendlike at times:
and the poor little child would catch its first notions
of life from the worst specimens of humanity. A
convict mother must entail misery on her offspring,
and we found that in Mountjoy Prison an attempt
was being made to mitigate the evil. All women
are by law allowed to have with them very young
children in the prison; if the sentence is long, the
poor child may have dreary years to spend in this

abode;—for what mercy would it bo to it to send it
forth into the world uncared for, unprovided for?
Hence this Infant School, to which we were now
conducted. It was not indeed as cheerful and happy
a looking place as we should like to see young
children in;—we could not but notice strong thick
walls outside the school-room, which spoke clearly
to us the dreadful word 'prison.' But the officials
told us that these poor little things were not conscious of their peculiar position, and did not consider
that they were in gaol, but in ' Mrs. Lidwell's workhouse,' as they called it. They looked cheerful,
happy, healthy, and clean, in their Sunday pinafores;
and their teacher seemed fond of them, and so did
the worthy Superintendent, Mrs. Lidwell; and they
certainly looked better and more cared for than did
the poor children we afterwards saw in one of the
Dublin workhouses. We were told, and readily
believed it, that it produced an excellent effect on
the mothers, who were unhappily there as convicts,
to know that their children were within reach, and
that if their conduct was good they would be allowed
the Sabbath privilege of having their young ones
under their own care for a time;—perhaps there
they first began to think of their solemn respon-
sibilities as mothers. Under existing circumstances,
this Infant School in a Convict Prison is good and
beneficial,—the best thing that can be done for the
child: but surely it ought not to be so. Surely no
young child should enter on life's training under such

a stigma as having been bred in a gaol!—surely
society should take care that its young members
should be properly educated somewhere, when the
parent is removed by the arm of the law;—surely a
workhouse school should be a more appropriate and
happy home than one in a gaol. It is not so at
present! May it be so ere long!

" We next visited Mountjoy on a week day. This
prison contains both the first and second stages of the
female convicts. In consideration of the greater
susceptibility of women, the time of entire separation
is four months instead of eight, conditional of course
on good conduct and industry; if these are not satisfactory, the time is extended. The general arrangements and system are similar to those of the men,
and through all is there the same individual
watchfulness and care, combined with strict regulations ; a sense of justice blending with all in the
mind of the prisoners. We visited the second stage,
the associated work-room, where a large number of
women were engaged in needlework, under superin-
tendence. It was well for them to have this occupation
to draw off their thoughts from themselves. One
hour in every day they receive a lesson in the school-
room. There we found intelligent schoolmistresses
engaged closely, each with a class which she received
in rotation. It was a strange sight to see elderly
women in spectacles standing in class, spelling out
the Irish lesson books, which are so familiar to our
children. But we were much astonished at the

proficiency which some, even of those, had made. We know the extreme difficulty which is experienced by young persons, who have been early neglected, in overcoming the mysterious combinations of letters into syllables, and the connection between these forms and the corresponding sounds. It was, therefore, a remarkable and significant fact, that only one hour a day, well and actively employed with real goodwill to learn, should have produced such results. The women greatly appreciate this hour's instruction; faculties before dormant are excited and exercised; and thoughts are opened to them which excite new ideas and aspirations. Some of the classes had attained considerable proficiency, and their teachers were evidently proud of them. More advanced stages of the women were engaged in various kinds of house-work and cooking, and a number in washing and ironing. These occupations seemed more calculated than the needlework to rouse their energies in a right direction, and to draw off their thoughts from themselves; consequently their countenances look better, and indeed as the stages advanced it was easy to trace an improvement in expression. Hard work is a most important element of training, and a great aid in subduing bad passions. One woman, of stalwart appearance, was working with great zeal at a washing-machine: she had been guilty of manslaughter! One shuddered to think of what she must have been capable when her passions were wild and unregulated. But though the

faces of many were bad, yet we could perceive, as
we advanced, a great softening of expression, and in
none did we observe that sullen, dogged, and rebel-
lious look, which indicates that the governed and the
governing party are not working harmoniously. The
most advanced at Mountjoy are placed in a 'prepa-
ratory class.'

"Now the establishment of an 'intermediate
stage' for women, corresponding to the Lusk and
Smithfield for men, was long a difficult and perplex-
ing problem. Yet it was necessary to solve it. Why
are the public unwilling to take into their employment
persons who have come straight from prison, however
good those prisons may be? Simply because they do
not believe in the reformation of the prisoners, and
with justice; for where the will is absolutely enthral-
led, it is impossible to tell how an individual will act
when the restraint is removed. It is one of the grand
secrets of the success of the Irish Convict Prisons,
which is acknowledged by all who personally study
the subject, that this principle is understood and
acted on. But the women could not with safety be
allowed the same liberty as the men. Not only would
the difference in character to which we have alluded
prevent this, but the dangers of the streets to females,
especially of this class, would render such liberty
most unsuitable. Under these perplexities, the
Directors availed themselves of the voluntary zeal
and devotion which offered to take charge of the
women who should be considered worthy of the

privilege of an intermediate stage. The nuns of
Golden Bridge, who had already considerable experience in the care of a Penitentiary, undertook the
charge of such Catholic convict women as should be
sent to them. They are there still under their
sentence of detention, and subject, as at Lusk and
Smithfield, to be sent back to Mountjoy should their
conduct prove unsatisfactory, and they are under the
constant inspection of the Directors; but, in other
respects, they are under the management of the nuns.
There we saw them, and remarked a most favourable
change in their appearance and deportment; indeed
had we not been aware that they were convicts, we
should not have imagined it from anything we
observed. The women were chiefly engaged in
laundry-work, cheerfully and actively. We con-
versed with several of them, and found them all
anxious to lead a new life, and preparing for it.
Golden Bridge has large grounds connected with it,
which afford to the women the salutary influences of
out-door occupation; there are the garden and potato-
ground to be cultivated, and the pigs and poultry to
be attended to; the care of animals is generally
beneficial, and intercourse with nature always is so.
These, combined with the religious and moral influences exercised by the nuns, and their Christian
interest in them, afford an excellent preparation for
future life. There is also a Protestant institution of
a similar kind in Heytesbury Street, superintended
by ladies; the number here is small, but the same

object is in view ; and here, as at Golden Bridge, the
ladies who undertake the charge keep a friendly
watchfulness over the women when discharged.
The plan has answered admirably. The women
fully appreciate the kindness which is shown them,
and the efforts which are made for their good,
and they go forth again to the world in a very
different position from what they could have done
from any prison. The public, too, place confidence
in the characters which they receive from the ladies
who have the management of these institutions, and
know to what influences they have been subjected.
Hence they are not unwilling to receive these women
into domestic service ; and many are satisfactorily
placed out, while others emigrate. This plan has
not been in operation as long as the Intermediate
Prison for men, but hitherto it has answered admirably and gives good promise. The same principle is
in operation here as at Lusk, and produces the same
results."

It is a sufficient proof of the efficiency of this
system, if worked in accordance with its intention
and principles, that of 510 female convicts who were
licensed during the seven years from 1856 to 1862
inclusive, only 21 had their licenses revoked for misconduct in the refuges, and 5 after ; in all 26, viz.,
5 per cent. Only 4 of the whole number were reconvicted, viz., 0·8 per cent., or less than one.

In Ireland, the public has fully coöperated in the
work undertaken by the managers of the refuges, in

restoring these women to society. Increased experience only confirms the truth of the principle on which they are founded. The ladies who take an interest in these refuges have full opportunity of judging of the competency of the women, and the sincerity of their reformation; they are, therefore, in a position to recommend them, and the public place confidence in their recommendation. The women also find themselves still, on their actual discharge, under the friendly surveillance of those who have already proved their true interest in them, by their earnest efforts for their reformation.

CHAPTER V.

THE foregoing chapters have, we trust, satifactorily proved that a truly reformatory system of prison discipline can effect the end intended, that of restoring criminals to society, and enabling them to enter the labour market as honest men. The Irish Convict Prisons as developed by Sir Walter Crofton did fulfil all the conditions required, and did attain the end intended.

Did these prisons, however, necessarily diminish the crime of the country? No statistics could possibly prove this;—if they appeared to do so, by a great decrease in the number of convicts, which was the case to a great extent, that decrease may be attributed to some other cause. All that can be done by the very best prisons is simply to reform the prisoners, and thus prevent them from adding to the crime of the country. This, the vigilant police supervision, and the careful registration of crime carried out in connection with the Irish Convict Prisons, were able to prove to be truly effected.—A hospital placed near an ill-drained district, a seed plot of disease and death, cannot render the district healthy. We must search out the causes of the evil, and employ sanitary measures to remedy the evil.—The same course should be pursued in dealing with crime. While we endeavour to reform offenders, we should, by wise methods of prevention, arrest their downward course before they become convicts.

We shall now, therefore, briefly consider the best means of checking the growth of crime in its earliest stages, and thus stop the supply of fresh convicts, to be maintained for many years at great expense in Government Prisons.

Most of the criminals of the country can trace out their first entrance into crime to a neglected youth.

Some will suppose that in countries where provision is made by the State for a free education, such cases should not occur. But those who are practically acquainted with the condition of the children who fill our Workhouses, Industrial Schools, and Reformatories, are well aware that they spring from a lower stratum of society than can be reached by any system of public education. It exists in New York and other cities of the United States where special agencies are required to meet the necessities of this class of children, though the excellent common schools close their doors against none. In all the large cities of England they are to be found.

The testimony of the present writer at the Birmingham Educational Conference of 1861 is, unhappily, still true:—

"To perceive the existence of this class, it is necessary only to walk, as I have done, through whole districts of Liverpool, endeavouring to discover among those squalid courts and alleys some of the families whence children have been rescued as brands from the burning, and sent to a Reformatory;—to go into the swarming by-streets of the old town of Warrington, and there find the wretched children so unaccustomed to even the casual notice of one of the civilised class, that they stared with astonishment when I addressed to them words of kindness. It needs but to walk, as I have, at all hours, through the Lewin's Mead district of Bristol, unhappily by no means unique in its character in that ancient city, to perceive the fearful evil, and see year after year pass without any material alteration in it. Decades of years glide by, and it is still the same. Half a century ago its infamous character was such that a respectable labouring man, whose road lay through it to convey a lady home on Sabbath evenings from her place of worship, declared that the language and scenes to which he was exposed made him feel as if he were going 'out of heaven into the bottomless pit.' When, some years ago, I gave a lessson to a Ragged School in this district on the destruction of Sodom, the wickedness and riot described in the Scripture narrative appeared to the children merely a portraiture of familiar scenes; and they all acknowledged that if Lewin's Mead had been the subject of the patriarch's prayer, to save it from destruction, not ten good men could be found here any more than there. Nine years ago I stated in my evidence before the Commons' Committee the condition of this part of the city, which is such as to render it seldom visited by the police, who dare not singly cope with so vicious a population. Within this very month, as I walked through it, the whole thoroughfare was crowded with combatants, leaving no space for passengers; and a policeman at hand angrily refused me to interfere, until supported by several others."

Such scenes as these are familiar to persons who are acquainted with the back slums of the metropolis.

Let us realise the consequence to the community of whole districts remaining in this state of isolated barbarism, and reflect how impossible it is for the children to emerge from it unhelped. Not only must they grow up to be no better than their parents, and perpetuate such a condition of things, but there is a constant tendency in them to drag down others from the class above them, whose natural dispositions or circumstances indicate a proclivity to crime. Workhouse Inspectors have long perceived the existence of this untaught and uncivilised class; from observing the condition of the inmates of the Workhouse, they have known that this class was not reached by the educational agencies of the country. This portion of our population is nearly untouched by any institutions of our country,—except the poorhouse, the police-force, and the gaol. They are in a state of semi-barbarism. They are slaves of their lower instincts and passions; they have no care for what does not immediately concern their present needs; nor will they sacrifice their convenience or their money to obtain education for their children, for they no more comprehend its true value than a man blind from birth can understand the nature of sight. They live in a state of ignorance of all that constitutes civilised society, a practical ignorance of man's immortal nature and destiny.

It is evidently useless to endeavour to bring children so reared into the ordinary elementary schools of the country. Not only would their presence be very unwelcome among the children of the working classes in such schools, but they themselves require something more than mere book learning, and unless this is supplied, no real improvement can be anticipated. For such children special schools must be provided.

Let it be supposed that all available means have been adopted by School Boards in our country, or by a general system of free education in others, to bring under good, simple education every child in the land; those of whom we have spoken will still remain untouched. Since neither they nor their parents have any desire to obtain education, they will be leading a lawless, vagrant life, the preparation for one of vagrancy and crime. Their homes, their habits, and their general condition is such that *compulsory attend-*

ance the WHOLE DAY, *in a school where they will be fed and taught industrial work and civilised as well as edu· cated intellectually, will* ALONE *meet their wants.*

Such schools have long been established in the north of England, and in Scotland, and answer the purpose admirably. In the county of Aberdeen, in the year 1844, 345 vagrant children were apprehended by the rural police. After a feeding Industrial Day School, with compulsory attendance, had been in operation for six months, the number fell in 1846 to fourteen, and they gradually dimished to two in 1850. The juvenile delinquents committed to gaol under twelve years of age fell from sixty-one in 1841 to twenty-one in 1850. In order to carry out the intention of this school and to act on the whole juvenile population, an office was established in the city of Aberdeen to which all children were brought who were wandering in the streets and otherwise uncared for, and after due inquiry they were sent to whatever school was most desirable. The same system was carried out in Edinburgh, and with similar success, under the leadership of the now venerable Dr. Guthrie, who has had the happiness of knowing that these feeding Industrial Day Schools have been the means of transforming thousands of misarable, half starved, vagabond children into honest self-supporting men and women, bringing up their children to be, like themselves, good citizens, instead of paupers and convicts. The principle of these schools was examined by the Select Committee of the House of Commons in 1852-53, who, in the 23rd section of their Report, expressed their opinion : — " That the Industrial Feeding Schools, at present supported by voluntary subscriptions, or, as in Glasgow, *by local rates*, have produced beneficial effects on the children of the most destitute classes of society inhabiting large towns."

We believe that it is only by such schools, where these wretched children can be brought during the greater part of the day under humanising influences, and taught what is necessary to enable them to do their duty to God and to man, that the source can be stopped from which a constant supply of paupers and convicts fill our workhouses and gaols.

Political economists may fear that bad parents will thus be encouraged in neglect. Let the law punish *them*, but let not the children suffer. Ratepayers may fear a small addition to their expenditure ;— they will be saved a much larger one in supporting whole families in workhouses.

Supposing such schools to be generally established in large cities, for the very lowest of the population, it will nevertheless be found that individuals of these are of too daring and headstrong a nature to be managed in simple Day Schools, and that some are found in other classes of society who, from various causes, are commencing a course of life which must lead on to crime. It is now a recognised principle in our country, that in such cases, parental authority not being sufficient to protect society from evils which these unrestrained children will bring upon them, this authority must bo forfeited and vested by tho Secretary of State with the managers of Industrial Schools, where the child is altogether boarded and cared for, and which aro *Certified* by him as fit and proper for the purposes. The State, now standing in *loco parentis* to the child, makes weekly allowance to the managers, which is supplemented by local rates and by voluntary contributions. The parent also is compelled, where possible, to contribute to the maintenance of his child. The intentions of the Act establishing these schools is shown by the following definitions of the children for whom it is intended :—

SEC. 14.—"Any person may bring before Two Justices or a Magistrate any Child, of either sex, apparently under the Age of Fourteen Years, that comes within any of the following Descriptions, namely,—

" That is found begging or receiving Alms (whether actually or under the pretext of selling or offering for Sale any Thing), or being in any Street or Public Place for the Purpose of so begging or receiving Alms ;

" That is found wandering and not having any Home or settled place of Abode, or proper Guardianship, or Visible Means of Subsistence ;

" That is found destitute, either being an Orphan or having a surviving Parent who is undergoing Penal Servitude or Imprisonment ;

" That frequents the Company of reputed Thieves.

" The Justices or Magistrate before whom a Child is brought as coming within One of those Descriptions, if satisfied on Inquiry of that Fact, and that it is expedient to deal with him under this Act, may order him to be sent to a Certified Industrial School."

15.—" Where a Child apparently under the Age of Twelve Years is charged before Two Justices or a Magistrate with an

H

Offence punishable by Imprisonment or a less Punishment, but
has not been in *England* convicted of Felony, or in *Scotland*
of Theft, and the Child ought, in the Opinion of the Justices or
Magistrate (regard being had to his Age and to the Circumstances of the Case) to be dealt with under this Act, the Justices
or Magistrate may order him to be sent to a Certified Industrial
School."

16.—" Where the Parent or Step-parent or Guardian of a
Child apparently under the age of Fourteen Years represents to
Two Justices or a Magistrate that he is unable to control the
Child. and that he desires that the Child be sent to an Industrial
School under this Act, the Justices or Magistrate, if satisfied on
Inquiry that it is expedient to deal with the Child under this
Act, may order him to be sent to a Certified Industrial School."

SEC. 17 provides that refractory children in Workhouses,
Pauper Schools, &c., if under 14 years old, may be sent to
Certified Industrial Schools.

SEC. 18 refers to the order of detention to be made by the
committing Justices, and concludes,—

" The Order shall specify the Time for which the Child is to
be detained in the School, being such Time as to the Justices or
Magistrate seems proper for the teaching and training of the
Child, but not in any case extending beyond the Time when the
Child will attain the Age of Sixteen Years."

Certified Industrial Schools have been in operation for about fourteen years; both official reports
and the general verdict of the public, prove that they
have had a great effect in arresting the course of
juvenile crime.

The essential element of success in the Certified
Industrial Schools has been the voluntary effort
which has been enlisted in the movement. Personal
interest has been excited in the managers for the

young boys or girls committed to their charge; this has been warmly returned by the scholars, with a grateful sense of benefits which money could not purchase, and has been a stimulus to self-improvement. Thus the good effects of the years spent in these schools have not ceased with the period of their detention there, but have followed them into the world where they have received a helping hand forward, from those of a higher class who now felt an individual interest in them.

Unhappily the same influences do not exist in Workhouse Schools, unless in rare and exceptional cases;—hence the poor children are not able to take in after life an honourable position in society, and the statement is true now which was made many years ago to the Lords' Committee by the Ordinary of Newgate, that "there is a close connection between the scum of a Workhouse and juvenile offenders." The general voice of the public assigns to the Workhouse boy or girl one of the lowest places in the community.

Nor is this the fault of the poor children. The Assistant Commissioner, Mr. Cumin, thus speaks of the Workhouse Schools which came under his observation, "I know nothing more pathetic than a Workhouse School. * * * Doomed by necessity never to know the meaning of the familiar word home—cut off from the exercise of the ordinary affections—many of them diseased in body and feeble in mind—these poor children exhibit little of the vigour and joyousness of youth. *Listless and subservient in manner, they seem to be broken down by misfortune before they have entered into life.*" The evil perpetuates itself.

The late Mr. Nassau Senior, one of the Educacation Commissioners, speaks thus of the Workhouse at Southampton, which he visited, " The paupers, they (the master and mistress) said, are a tribe, the same names, from the same families and the same streets fill the Workhouse; it sometimes contains three generations !"

These poor children have done nothing to deserve they too frequently receive, even without any conscious neglect of duty on the part of those under whose care they are placed. Nor can the present state of things be altered under the existing system of Poor Law regulations.

The pauper stamp is impressed on young children who ought to be rising freely into life ;—they have a sense of bondage ; they are cut off from ordinary life, and their ignorance of it makes them enter it unprepared, from schools which might be otherwise good. They cannot possess property, for paupers have none, and this deprives them of the possibility of learning some of the most important lessons to fit them for society. How can an orphan child brought up in a Workhouse School know what are the rights and duties of property ; the use and value of money ;

tho necessity of providence and economy to maintain an independent position in the world? He must, therefore, go forth into it unprepared!

All those children who are dependent on the parochial rates for support, ought, if they have a home, to be sent to the Day Feeding Industrial Schools, the payment allowed for their support being made over to the managers of the schools; if they require a home also, they should be placed in Certified Industrial Schools, the same sum being paid for the parish Guardians for their support as is paid to in other cases by the Secretary of State. Should no Certified Industrial School be available for the purpose, then similar schools should be established for them, under the management of a Board chosen by the ratepayers. For the development of such a system the following suggestions were offered by the present writer in evidence to the Poor Law Committee of 1861 :—

First.—It should be made unlawful for any children under sixteen years of age to be taken into the Workhouse, or any establishment connected with the Workhouse within three miles of it.

Secondly.—The management of all pauper children should be placed in the hands of a School Committee, to be annually chosen by the ratepayers. The school for girls must be under the immediate management of a Committee of ladies.

Thirdly.—All schools intended for resident pauper children should be certified as fit and proper for their purpose by the Secretary of State, to whom their condition should be annually reported, and who should have power to withdraw the certificate.

Fourthly.—Where no school exists in any district fit for the reception and proper training of pauper children, the Gurdians should vote a sum for the erection and suitable furnishing of one, under the direction of the School Committee.

Fifthly.—The Guardians should pay to the School Committee a weekly sum, not more than 5s., for the entire maintenance and instruction of each pauper child.

Sixthly.—All Pauper Schools must be industrial in their character ; should the School Committee think fit, the Pauper Industrial School may be certified by the Secretary of State for the reception of vagrant children, under the regulations of the Industrial Schools' Act. In like manner any School Committee may contract with the Managers of a Certified Industrial School to receive pauper children with the payment from the Guardians of 5s. a week.

On such a system the enlightened and benevolent effort of the country would be enlisted in the work of raising the children of paupers, and the destitute orphans of England, into a self-supporting and independent position ; one great seed-plot of crime would thus be thoroughly cleared.

A system of boarding out pauper children in respectable families, and cottage homes, has been adopted in many parts of the country with great success, where there has been a suitable Committee to undertake the oversight of them.

Were such institutions as we have here described, supplementing a good system of National Education, brought to bear on all the juvenile part of the population of our country, there can be no doubt that very few cases would occur in which young persons of the middle and lower classes would be found injuring society by the commission of crime, any more than those of the higher classes. But these are comparatively of recent date. A quarter of a century ago the gaols of our country were swarming with young criminals; — destined to cost the country large sums of money and to do immense injury to the moral tone of the country before their career was ended. It was then, the first work of the Reformatory movement, which commenced with the Birmingham Conference of December, 1851, to awaken the country and the Government to the necessity of providing Reformatory Schools for convicted juveniles instead of plunging them as heretofore in a career of crime. The revelations made to the public at that Conference were appalling. It was proved that gangs of young thieves were common; multitudes of boys and even girls, were found in all large towns, who had been six or eight times in prison, and were already adepts in crime. The experience of the United States, France, and other countries of Europe, proved that well managed Reformatories can arrest the progress of juvenile crime, and turn young delinquents into honest citizens.

In August, 1854, the first Reformatory Act was passed ;—that and subsequent ones were consolidated in 1866. This Act is permissive and experimental; it gives the power to all Magistrates, Recorders and Judges, to sentence to these Reformatory Schools children who have committed any act punishable with not less than fourteen days of previous imprisonment, but does not require them to do so; it leaves the establishment of these Schools to voluntary bene-volence; they are to be inspected by some person appointed by the Secretary of State, and on being certified by him as fit and proper for the purpose, children may be sentenced to them by Magistrates or Judges for a certain number of years.

The School remains under the sole direction of the voluntary managers; but the Secretary of State may examine it by his inspector at any time he pleases; if the state of the School is not satisfactory he may withdraw the certificate, and the School then ceases to be a Reformatory School under the meaning of the Act. The Secretary of State thus acts in *loco parentis* to the child, and when placing him in a School satisfies himself that it is well suited to his training.

The Secretary of State makes a grant for a fixed sum per head for each child sentenced to the School, as long as he is in it. In addition to this, counties or boroughs may, if they think fit, raise a county rate, and make an agreement with the managers of any School to contribute towards its support.

The Secretary of State has the power of discharging the child at any time; this is frequently done when the managers make application on the score of good conduct. The manager of the School may grant a license to any inmate, half of whose time of detention has expired, to be at large on trial, under the responsibility of the School.

The parents of the children are compelled to pay whatever may be ordered by the Magistrates towards the expense of the child while in the School, and this contribution relieves the treasury.

This is a general outline of the conditions under which children are placed in Reformatory Schools.

These schools have fully answered the expectations of those who commenced the movement. There is no longer organised juvenile crime in the country. We now rarely meet with a boy or a girl who has been in prison twice before committal to a Reformatory. We know that numbers of our old scholars have become respectable men and women, and heads of families who are brought up in a very different way from that in which they passed their early years. We know that very few of our old scholars have found their way into Convict Prisons. We trust that when they do, they will be subjected to Reformatory Prison discipline.

There is, however, another class of children, who, though not coming under the provisions of the Industrial Schools Act, and as yet unconvicted of crime, and, therefore, not fit for Reformatories, require to be placed in such institutions, if they are to be rescued from a life of crime. These are the children of convicts or habitual criminals who are certain to be trained in vice, if they are not removed from the custody of their relations, and placed under moral influence. This is a most important matter. It has been proved by experience that the children of criminals, who are not destitute and do not come under the law, are being trained by relations and friends in the paths of their parents. In the "Habitual Criminals' Act" is a clause stating that the children of habitual criminals might be sent to Industrial Schools; this was not, however, sufficiently stringent. The "Prevention of Crime Act," which became law during the last Parliamentary Session, has, in its fourteenth clause, materially amended former legislation on this subject, and we may now feel justified in assuming, that the State will henceforward perform the very important duty of sending to Industrial Schools, those who would otherwise assuredly recruit our criminal ranks.

The Red Hill Reformatory was originally established, under the name of the Philanthropic Society, more than eighty years ago, for the rescue of the children of convicts. The principle worked satisfactorily, and it is well that the Government should now endorse the principle that crime is to be prevented, by *absolutely* placing all such children in schools under legal detention.

CHAPTER VI.

STRINGENT and other measures for controlling the criminal classes have been repeatedly urged by Sir Walter Crofton, during the last fourteen years, in his various reports and pamphlets, as to police supervision, licenses, registration, prison systems, &c., as forming part of a whole. A few of these points will now be noticed, though space will not permit more than a very brief indication of some of the most important topics, connected with the repression of crime in a country.

In the first place, there should be a general and uniform system of the registration of criminals. Careful records may be, indeed, kept of the number of committals and convictions, but this gives no information respecting the number of individuals who have been engaged in criminal acts, still less does it indicate the number of recommittals and reconvictions. From time to time an experienced eye may detect the same individual as an old offender, and sagacious efforts may lead to discovery of the antecedents of the culprit. But at present there is no recognised and established means of ascertaining these.

Mr. Weatherhead, Governor of Holloway Prison, states to the Commission :--" There is," he says, " extreme difficulty in discovering previous convictions, particularly in the old incorrigible thief, or the clever thief. He escapes the former conviction better than a man who has been seldom in prison, and that class generally travel from county to county, or from one prison to another, and their former convictions are never brought to light against them." Out of the twenty or thirty whom Mr. Weatherhead ascertained to have been in Convict Prisons only about four were known at their trial to have been previously under sentence of penal servitude.

We have seen that in the Irish Convict System photography was found a most valuable help in this.

Secondly, there should be certainty in judicial sentences. The very different punishment awarded to the same offences by different judges, has a most injurious effect on the public mind, and especially on that of the criminal class. Sir Richard Mayne's opinion is founded on a long experience as Commissioner of the Metropolitan Police, since the foundation of the force in 1829, and is therefore very important. He says in his evidence before the Royal Commission in 1863 :—" I believe it is not too strong a word to use to say that the administration of the law with regard to the widely varying degrees of punishment at the present day is a scandal. Some of the judges, I think, pass sentences of eighteen months for an offence that another judge would pass a sentence of five years or more of penal servitude. The law gives them almost unlimited discretion whether they will pass a very long sentence of penal servitude, or a very short sentence of imprisonment; that latitude is universally 'large. This makes sentences perfectly uncertain and a species of lottery; *the police consider it so;* they often report to me with regard to a case,— So-and-so will be tried before such a Judge, and he will get a very light punishment."

The third improvement here suggested is, that sentences should be cumulative;—that is, that a frequent repetition of offences, though not themselves serious, should be followed by long reformatory treatment.

The reason and justice of this seems obvious. If a person is pursuing a course of conduct which is contrary to law and injurious to society, and if repeated punishments fail to produce any effect, or to check the individual in his vicious career, the perseverance in such illegal course, and, as it may be regarded, defiance of law, ought itself to be regarded as a crime involving a long course of punishment and reformatory treatment. It is almost impossible to calculate the evil to society caused by the presence of individuals who thus live in a manner regardless of law; the evil to the individual is not less of allowing him to continue such a course, and thus become callous to the disgrace and punishment of the gaol; and the cost to the public of his continual apprehensions, convictions and imprisonments, is far more than his incarceration in a prison, where he would be made to earn a portion, at least, of the cost of his maintenance.

As the law at present stands the same person is sentenced repeatedly, becomes habituated to a month's imprisonment in a gaol where his comforts are attended to, and he returns to his old haunts and associates, nothing daunted.

The principle of cumulative punishment would be particularly important in its influence on the female sex of the criminal class. When a woman has once undergone imprisonment she has lost her position in society, feels herself degraded, and becomes more and more reckless and hardened until she enters the Convict Prison. Rev. J. Morgan, Chaplain of Brixton Convict Prison, states in his evidence before the Commission that it is generally after repeated confinement in the County Prisons that women are sent to the Government Prisons. Some have had 14, and some as many as 40 previous convictions. One woman from Liverpool had had 47 convictions, and when she now received a long sentence of penal servitude, it was not in consequence of the previous convictions, but on account of the nature of her crime.

This view is strongly confirmed by the results of such a system in Liverpool, and the resolutions of the magistrates founded on that experience, as stated in a report issued in the present year. After noticing a very remarkable diminution in the number of indictable offences during the preceding year, they say : " The following causes of this have been the most influential :—

" 1st.—The more complete methods adopted of late years for ascertaining the past history of prisoners charged with felonies, for distinguishing the old from the casual offenders, and to the severity with which old offenders are now punished; in other words, to the greater extend to which the cumulative principle of punishment is applied in the sentences passed on those found repeatedly guilty of the more serious kinds of crime.

" 2ndly.—The greater severity which has lately characterized the discipline of the convict and other prisons.

" 3rdly.—The aid given to discharged convicts and prisoners by the Discharged Prisoners' Aid Societies and other kindred agencies, and to the Police supervision exercised over suspicious characters under the Habitual Criminals Act.

" These causes have combined on one hand to make the penal consequences of a career of crime very intolerable, and on the other hand to offer to prisoners willing to abandon it greater facilities for earning a respectable living. The decrease in the number of serious crimes has taken place just at the time when the action of the causes referred to might have been expected to produce this result."

After giving a table showing the large number of reconvictions of the same individuals, from 15 to 70 times, they continue :—

"The Committee are of opinion that the preceding analysis of the sources from whence the prison is filled, and especially the figures as shown in Table IV., point strongly to the conclusion that *the cumulative principle of punishment* should, with greater or less severity, be consistently applied to all offences; —that is to say, that the punishments should gradually be increased, if offences are very often repeated by the same individual. There are many persons on whom a succession of sentences of short or intermediate length has absolutely no effect; indeed, when bad habits have taken root for years, and when all power of self-controul has been destroyed by a long course of self-indulgence, it is vain to expect a sentence of three or even twelve months to lead to an altered life; on the other hand, experience already quoted, of the results of the long sentences with which repeated offences of the more heinous kinds have of late years been visited, does appear to show that they often produce a good effect when shorter ones have failed. The Committee believe that favorable results would also follow if the cumulative principle were applied as consistently, though in a milder way to the secondary kinds of offences.

"Long sentences are not only often feared by those who have become callous to short ones, and are therefore deterrent, but they aid persons who have found a criminal or disorderly life wretched, to abandon it. The long detention away from customary temptations gives them time to eradicate bad associations, while it also generally gives time for the bands of bad companions to which they may have belonged to break up and disperse, and often thus saves them from being led back into bad ways by old associates.

A remarkable history, which strikingly confirms all the foregoing principles, both preventive and corrective, occurs in the recently issued report of the Prison Association of New York for 1872—p. 48. It is here extracted, because it admirably illustrates the evil of the want of correction at the commencement of a criminal course, and the importance of careful police supervision to discover crime, and long reformatory prison discipline to change the character :—

"In a county jail in the Western part of the State the Secretary's inspection brought before him a young man who had served a full term of imprisonment in the Auburn State Prison, and a term in the Eastern Penitentiary of Pennsylvania, and who had been an inmate of numerous jails, always for crimes against property, horse-stealing, larcenies of goods, dealing in counterfeit money, and forgeries—and, at the time of this examination, again under arrest for his *chef-d'œuvre* of crime, namely, stealing a valuable horse. And he confessed to the writer that he had stolen five horses during the previous six months, without having been suspected, as he believes, excepting in the last theft, which he committed in a border county State, from the Governor of which a requisition has been sent for him.

"With a third term of punishment in State prison before him, this young criminal, at the close of a private interview with him, stated with entire simplicity and apparent penitence that, as the law had now got fast hold of him, he would endeavor

I

to break away from every practice and associate in crime. The following is an abstract of the statements made by this prisoner in the interview mentioned, as far as they have been verified:—

"*Personal History.*—M—— says he has been a criminal ever since he was eleven years of age. His father is a business man in L. R., where the prisoner was born, twenty-seven years ago.

"His mother died when he was only eight years of age, and after that his care and government were capricious, and his temper petulant and at times reckless. When eleven years of age his truant habits brought him in the company of a young thief who had suffered the jail penalty for his larcenies, and he taught and persuaded him to steal from his father's cash-box at the business office. This he repeated successfully, and finally was detected and punished by his father, and from that time was tauntingly termed the thief by father and workmen. His truancy became village vagrancy, and at fourteen he absconded from home and became a pedlar of trinkets. Again at home he was indolent, and aped the gentleman loafer. At the age of eighteen he stole a valuable horse in E., N. Y.; and, when arrested, was bailed, and the offence compromised and condoned by the father. The next year he abandoned home and joined himself to the fortunes of an ex-convict in a large gang of professional criminals. By that prison-graduate he was introduced to three very adroit and yet unpunished contrivers and teachers of crime in Ontario county, and also to the infamous Sims, of Belle Isle, near Camillus, Onondaga county. He found Sims an expert teacher concerning counterfeit money and its movements, and he found that the Ontario county men (keepers of canal-stables and drams-shops) were adepts in a great variety of crimes that require contrivance, such, for example, as the "shoving" of counterfeit currency; the packing and transportation of stolen goods; the stealing and disguising of horses, and secreting and sale of them; and the disguising and sale of stolen carriages, saddles, etc.; and, particularly, the instruction and subordination of canal and railroad employés in extensive larcenies and the "shoving" of counterfeit money.

"Pursuing his career of crime against property, he had occasion frequently to supply himself with counterfeit money in the city of New York, which he obtained on easy terms at ——— in Centre street. But before a year of this professional crime in its varied forms had elapsed, he was arrested in the State of Pennsylvania, and sentenced to the Eastern Peniten-tiary for a term of eighteen months in solitary confinement.

"At the expiration of his sentence he bounded into free life, elated with the idea that he had become a truly religious man; and having prepossessing manners, he at once obtained employment in a rural village, and became a Sabbath teacher, but soon fell into temptation, forged notes, and, after various escapades from arrest, he again became a horse-thief. In September, 1868, he stole a horse in the town of S., in ——— county, N. Y., and was proved guilty, and sentenced to the State prison for two years and eight months.

"In prison he was a pet, and lived at ease, playing at waiter upon the warden, etc. He asserts he had no consciousness of punishment or penalty, nor any wish to escape from this impri-sonment. He wrote to the Prison Association for some good place of employment, but when released he plunged headlong into temptations and bad associations; and after marrying a wife in a respectable family, he pursued his vocation as a horse-thief, forger, and dealer in counterfeit money. Some of the horses he had stolen during the last six months were yet unsold, and were being kept in distant localities, awaiting his antici-pated opportunities and movements. In recounting to the writer the methods and individuals that most aided him, he mentioned eleven men, who are expert horse-thieves and recei-vers of stolen goods. Most of the men he mentioned carry on active business, exchange and speculate freely in property of various kinds, and every one of them is reputed among his neighbors grossly immoral and unworthy of public confidence. They reside in different counties, between Delaware and Alle-gany counties, and whether acquainted with each other or not, were all well known to this young horse-thief, and were always ready to aid in secreting both the thief and his booty, and are known to be proud of their renown among thieves.

"It is not the purpose of this partial outline of an individual criminal's early career to bring forward any other than the points which chiefly relate *to the most preventable methods by which habits of criminal character are established, and the destructive forces of professional crime are seductively and fatally worked.*"

To effect a great change in an individual is necessarily a work of time, as we have seen when tracing the development of the Crofton system, and though it is certain that the system, being founded on sound principles is applicable to all countries, for offenders under long sentences, yet it may appear doubtful whether it can be applied to ordinary gaols, for short sentenced prisoners.

It will therefore be valuable to learn the experience in confirmation of this possibility, which was laid before the Social Science Association, held in London in 1862. Mr. Sheppard, the Governor of Wakefield Gaol, thus spoke:—

"We cannot be told that it is impossible to reform the adult and hardened criminal ; we know what has been done in Ireland, and what has been done there can be done elsewhere.

"Limited as we are by the present conditions of the law, the Visiting Justices resolved to try in the West Riding Prison an experiment which should introduce such of the Irish System as under the circumstances could be appropriated.

"This alteration in the discipline was introduced in November last, and I will limit myself to such statements as will simply illustrate the working and the general principle sought to be carried out.

"All convicted prisoners on their reception are placed in the probation class on the lowest diet, and kept as strictly separate as the law will allow.

"After 14 days of continued good conduct some alteration is made in the severity of the discipline, a different employment and out-door exercises are given. These slight relaxations are intended to show the prisoner that he has advanced one step.

"After a further probation of a month's continued good conduct, other indulgences are granted in increased exercise, a greater variety of books, educational instruction, and an improved dietary. This latter seems solely an animal one, but it must be considered that those to whom it is applied are often little better than animal beings, whose appetites have the principal rule over them, and if we can induce these to subserve their moral good we are turning them to a worthy use. This privilege of better dietary is likewise requisite when we recollect that for the lowest class the minimum has been given (or rather, I should say, ought to be given) that is compatible with health, and that the active employment in labour in the next classes requires also an improved diet.

"The machinery by which a prisoner raises himself from a lower to a higher class is the same as we saw in active operation in Ireland, namely, the system of marks. By this system a prisoner is no longer treated in the mass, his individual character comes under observation. A notice is given to him shewing the indulgences he will receive on his advancement to the next higher class, and an explanation of the marks, by what such advance can be obtained.

"A prisoner soon understands and appreciates the value of these marks, and when he finds he has received only one mark for his work, he at ones determines to exert himself to gain more, and as my daily experience shews, he takes especial care that no mistake is made against himself.

" It is when I come to speak of results, that I must apologize
to the section for introducing an experiment to their notice
which has been for so short a time in operation. The first
noticeable fact is an increase in the labour of the prisoners, but
the most observable effect of the experiment is the improved
conduct of the prisoners.

" The average number of misconduct reports of a nature so
slight as to require only a caution, was in the year 1860, 140 per
month on population of 500, or 25 per cent. In the five months
in 1862, that is since the introduction of this new dicipline,
there have been 106 reports per month of a like nature on a
population, averaging 695, or 15 per cent., but it is when the
prison offences are repeated, or when they are of a more serious
nature, requiring actual prison punishment, that the great difference of conduct shews itself. In the year 1861, 91 prisoners
were punished monthly, or 16 per cent. on the population, and
since January last 41 per month, or only 6 per cent. have been
punished.

" The good effects of the new discipline are shown
markedly by the progressive decrease in punishments monthly.
In January last 84 prisoners were punished, in February 40, in
March 43, in April 25, and in May only 14, and this on a population of above 700."

It cannot be stated that Winchester Gaol is
exactly on this system, but like some other gaols, it
has, like the instance above cited, adopted as its
ruling principle one of the most important features
in it, viz., a *progressive system of classification* governed
by "marks," which are earned by the prisoners,
and it therefore depends upon themselves to ameliorate their condition morally and materially.

The Chaplain of Winchester Gaol (Rev. F.
Rogers) in his report for 1866, states :—" In the

year *previous to the introduction of the mark system* there were 721 reports in two divisions of the prison. This year there have been only 297 in the same divisions. It is hardly necessary to add this indicates a proportionate increase in the industry, as well as the orderly conduct of the prisoners."

At present, however, there is unfortunately a great *want of uniformity* in our prison treatment. Considering the experience which has now been attained, and the general unanimity of opinion which prevails upon the subject, it is of the utmost importance that the Government should take the necessary steps to promote it.

It is evident that to carry out this reformatory system or any part of it, the gaol premises should be of such a nature as to secure separate confinement absolutely in the early stage of imprisonment, with separate cells for sleeping in the second. The old system of association in gaol has now been discontinued in our country. It was well known to produce universally most injurious results, and to cause a great increase of crime. In one such gaol at Liverpool, the Select Committee of the House of Lords in 1847 reports, "The evidence gives a frightful picture of the effects produced by the contamination of a gaol. In Liverpool, of fourteen cases, selected at random by the magistrates, there were several of the boys under twelve who in the space of three or four years had been above fifteen times committed; and the average of the whole fourteen was no less than nine

times." On the 4th of February, 1856, there were
in that gaol 91 boys boys; ten only had not been
previously in gaol; the remaining 81 had an average
of three convictions each. In that gaol every possible moral influence was used for there formation
of the prisoners, but nothing could prevent the
contamination caused by the association of the
wicked with each other. No one can tell how many
henious crimes have been planned in gaols, how
many prisoners have there learnt all the arts of house
breaking and garotting. It is to be hoped that the
knowledge of the subject disseminated widely through
the present International Congress, will lead to the
entire abandonment of such gaols as are described
in the recently issued report of the New York Prison
Association. Instances there mentioned (p. 9),
strikingly show the enormous evil done to society by
even one such place :—

"In one of the gaols on Long Island, containing at the time of inspection thirty-one prisoners, there were found five boys and young
men accused of burglary or attempt at that crime,
committed from different sections of the county; two
accused of rape; one of child murder; three others,
accused of misdemeanors, were insane and in a state
of mental imbecility; while petty larceny, assault
and battery, and disorderly conduct were enume-
rated as the offences for which the others were
committed.

"These prisoners were crowded promiscuously

into a filthy and dilapidated corridor and its adjoining dark cells, and in a rickety old chamber consisting of two dismal apartments opening into each other, and having grated windows that scarcely offer resistance to prisoners who may determine to break gaol. Herded together as those prisoners were, the Secretary of this Association deemed it expedient to advise the keeper to exercise special vigilance to prevent the burglars from escaping, and at the same time urged that the attention of the authorities be called to the insane and the imbecile persons whom he designated. Indictments and a formal 'gaol delivery' could not be had until two months had elapsed, and during that interval, when several professional criminals had been added to that motley crowd of prisoners, eight of the worst culprits,—including the five young burglars,—broke gaol and escaped. Such is the story of many a county gaol and of the successful escapes of the professional criminals, who under a wise system of administration ought never to pass through such an experience of eluding justice.

"In another gaol, in the western part of the State, always crowded with professional criminals and juvenile offenders, the Secretary of the Association found the prisoners in a state of feverish excitement as the result of plots for escaping, the old offenders stimulating the youths the least guilty to join not only in the plots to break gaol, but in schemes to commit future crimes. In another gaol two bright-eyed little boys, aged twelve and thirteen years respectively, accused of larcenies, were found sitting in the laps of two of the most accomplished and notorious burglars, learning not only the easy lessons of criminal life, but, as the lads confessed, learning the phrases and acquiring the habits of vice, while awaiting through a three months' interval the sitting of a grand jury and a criminal court.

"In another overcrowded gaol several of the untried culprits were in irons and dark cells, as a necessary restraint upon their efforts to break gaol; in their cells they were making an incessant uproar that disturbed the occupiers of several blocks of neighbouring dwellings; and as all classes of the prisoners were closely commingled in a central corridor, their days and nights were rendered intolerably wretched.

" In still another gaol, with seventy prisoners, many of them youths, all kinds of petty offenders were commingled with the most debased contrivers and actors in crimes,—mostly crimes against property. The sheriff showed our Secretary the freshly broken wall of the gaol through which a gang of desperadoes were, a few nights previously, about to escape. They would have succeeded, had not a penitent young man —under indictment for a homicide—given timely notice to the officers in charge.

" In another gaol, with an average of sixty-five prisoners in its cells and corridors, plots for breaking gaol are continually in progress, and are easily executed, as the record of escapes the past ten years would show. These plots, and the capricious severity that follows upon their discovery; the adroit and seductive instruction in the schemes of criminal life; the commingling of all classes of prisoners, produce together a total amount of evil and of personal debasement which is equalled only by *the terrible retribution by which the State is repaid for its neglect of the criminal classes—a neglect whereby crimes are multiplied and criminals made more daring as well as more corrupt.*"

Not only in the Western, but in the Eastern Hemisphere the fundamental necesssity of separate cells in the first stage of prison discipline is not yet understood, and the principles on which it rests are not universally accepted. In the great empire of India there is probably not one gaol adapted to the separation of prisoners. Dr. Mouat, late Inspector General of Prisons in Lower Bengal, has in his various official reports pointed out the enormous evils, both moral and physical, which have arisen in that country from a want of the proper construction of gaols, and the association of prisoners both by day and by night. In a paper recently read before the Statistical Society of London, Dr. Mouat says, " To place the prisons of Bengal on the footing required by our present knowledge of the subject needs the reconstruction of most of them. All Convict Prisons or Central Gaols should be *entirely on the separate system*, and proper means of separating prisoners should be provided in all District Prisons. Adequate establishments to work them efficiently should be given to all. The Central (or convict) Gaols now in course of construction in Bengal, fall very far short of these requirements, and *I regard them as a waste of public money.*"

Associated Gaols are worse than merely useless. They are nurseries for crime of the most dangerous kind. When loose in the world, the ill-disposed do not necessarily come into close personal contact with the wicked ; there are other influences around them, other occupations, other objects of thought, and the check of public opinion. In the Associated Gaol, the very atmosphere is polluted ; — public opinion in favour of evil,—the surroundings are such as to fill the mind and heart with corrupt imaginings and desires ;—deprived of liberty, brought into the closest contact, from which there is no escape, those weak in virtue become strong in vice, and inspired on entering the world with an intense feeling of shame, or perhaps vindictive defiance, the bond is loosened which held them to society, and they do what they can to injure it. Those who have already plunged into a vicious life plan together future crimes, to be accomplished with greater knowledge, and more power of evil when once at liberty. The crime of every country must be increased by every such gaol which exists in it. The infection of vice spreads as surely and certainly as of the plague ! May this world-wide Congress spread into every country the knowledge of the evil, and may public opinion never cease to influence governments until such schools of vice as Associated Schools are is removed from every civilized country on the earth !

(The Crofton system of convict treatment has been proved to have fulfilled all the objects of punishment. It gives suffering for evil doing, and encouragement to self-improvement; it rouses the offender to independent action, under the controul of law and duty, it excites in him a feeling of goodwill towards those under whose controul he is placed, by showing him that they are pursuing a course which will tend to his good, and that they are acting from a sense of duty. It finally restores him to society. It is thus Reformatory Prison Discipline.)

Supposing, however, that all places of penal confinement were so constructed, and on such a system, as to be truly reformatory—and calculated therefore to minimise the crime of the country;—there would still be needed external voluntary effort to aid the convict in restoration to society. Such, we saw, was the establishment at Golden Bridge in Dublin, from which the Lady Superior is able at the present day to declare that thousands have been restored to society as honest women. A similar institution has been established by Sir Walter Crofton, with the consent and coöperation of the Government, in connection with the English Female Convict Prisons.

The difficulty in England of developing any refuges similar to those in Ireland, which have been described in Chapter IV., appeared from various causes almost insurmountable. Happily, however, in 1865 all obstacles were removed, and the "Carlisle Refuge for Female Convicts" was established. The following are the grounds on which it was based :—

1st.—That as there are much greater difficulties to overcome in the way of obtaining employment for female than male convicts, it is imperative that some exceptional aid should be afforded to them, the more especially as the increasing stringency of pro- cedure with regard to our criminal classes renders it necessary that the well intentioned should have their good resolutions aided by every possible means

2nd.—That the women can be better prepared for release in the Refuge than in prison, and that their employment, on liberation, can thus be materially aided.

3rd.—That the Royal Commissioners on Penal Servitude in their report urged the importance of such an institution.

4th.—That the system has been pursued in Ire- land for very many years with the greatest advantage.

5th.—That the Government coöperated with the Committee, and agreed to send to the Refuges female convicts under certain regulations.

6th.—That the Committee propose to name the institution the " CARLISLE MEMORIAL REFUGE," in order to show their high appreciation of the services of the late Earl of Carlisle in Criminal Reform.

Many doubts were expressed, whether, taking into consideration the extremely depraved and violent class of persons to be dealt with, it would be possible to maintain order in an establishment in which physical controul could not be exercised over the inmates. It was also stated that, supposing this difficulty to be overcome, it was not probable that persons knowing them to have been convicts would give them employment. All these difficulties however have been overcome.

The women are sent out on license to the Refuge six months prior to their conditional liberation— misconduct in the establishment would cause them to be returned to the prison. But during seven years only two have been so returned.

Alluding to the recent establishment of another Female Convict Refuge in England (the Westminster Refuge), and to the desire of the Liverpool Justices to establish "Homes" in connection with County and Borough Gaols, the Refuge report for 1871 says,— " When it is remembered that not many years since, notwithstanding that the principle had been adopted in Ireland for a considerable period, very great fears were expressed that the institution of any " Home " for the reception of such a degraded class as female convicts in England would assuredly result in disorder and disappointment, it is highly satisfactory to those connected with the establishment of the "Carlisle Memorial Refuge," and those who have assisted in its management, that its success has been the means of extending its principles."

Many Prisoners' Aid Societies have been established both in the metropolis and in various large cities. These have been of very great benefit, both in aiding prisoners from common gaols who have been discharged, and in coöperating with the police in the supervision of convicts on license.

But in many other ways benevolent effort must coöperate if crime is to decrease in our country. The chief moving cause of it is drunkenness. To this great evil all judges and magistrates can testify. The late excellent Chaplain of Preston Gaol, Rev. John Clay, bore testimony to this in a petition which he drew up from the written statements of eighty prisoners, and which was signed by 247 prisoners, and was presented to the House of Lords:—

" That your Petitioners have had painful experience of the miseries, bodily and spiritual, produced by beer-houses, and are fully assured that those places constitute the greatest obstacles to the social, moral and religious progress of the labouring classes. They are alike injuries to old and young. By frequenting them parents bring their families to disgrace and ruin, and children are familiarised with vice nd crime. They combine whatever is demoralising in the ale-house, pawn-shop, fence-shop, gaming-house and brothel. Your Petitioners have all been drawn, by frequenting beer-houses, into offences and crimes of which they might otherwise have remained innocent. We speak from our own direct and bitter knowledge, when we declare that beer-houses lead to Sabbath-breaking, blasphemy, fraud, robbery, stabbings, manslaughters and murders !"

All houses known to be maintained for immoral purposes abound in large towns, and others where the disposal of stolen property is made easy; these ought to be under controul, if they cannot be actually suppressed. In a police report of Liverpool for 1865 it appears that there were 1,473 houses of bad character within the borough. What wonder then if crime abounds there? Can no legislation correct this?

In Great Britain, we believe that this great evil is fully acknowledged and has been removed from our penal discipline. Much progress has been made in many ways during the last ten years, in enlightening the public mind, and in introducing into the legislature laws for the prevention of crime and repression of habitual crime. All the efforts that have been made by the Government and by the public, have combined on one hand to make the penal consequences of a career of crime very intolerable, and on the other hand to offer to prisoners willing to abandon it greater facilities for earning a respectable living. The decrease in the number of serious crimes has taken place just at the time when the action of the causes referred to might have been expected to produce this result.

It was stated by Mr. Bruce, the Home Secretary, in the House of Commons, on the 16th Feb., 1872, "that the legislation for habitual criminals was having a striking and almost unexpected effect in diminishing the number of inverate criminals, the most experienced Judges having remarked at the assizes that they had never known so few persons

K

tried for repeated offences." This official testimony is gratifying, but we must not "rest," there is much to be done yet in our country. May we never cease our efforts until every measure has been adopted which is needed for the diminution of crime in the land.

Demoralising literature has a most powerful influence to evil. Mr. Clay gives the following statement of a young man sentenced to transportation :—

"At about 13 years of age, I began to read *The Newgate Calendar, and all such books as these, Jack Sheppard, Turpin, and different kinds of romances;* this, with the *advice of wicked men, made me inclined to follow some of their examples, and to try if I could not imitate some of their evil deeds.* * * In a short time I began to commit greater offences, one of which I got taken for, and got one month in prison at Salford House of Correction, which made me worse than ever, *through having so much liberty for talking by being three or four in a cell, and forty or fifty in a yard. The hearing them talk about the robberies they had committed, without being apprehended, I thought I would try myself.* So, when I got my liberty, I started with a fresh gang for a while."

A sound education and the providing of a pure and interesting class of books may correct this.

There are various important laws which have been made by the Legislature for the suppression of houses of ill-fame, receiving-houses of stolen goods, and others of an immoral character, which remain virtually a dead letter through want of coöperation on the part of society in carrying them into effect. It is evidently the intention of the Legislature that no direct incitements to be evil should be tolerated. Yet all these criminal resorts and open allurements to sin flourish among us, and remain unblushingly in our midst in the face of the day. They must be connived at, or this could not still continue to be the case. Every one who knows of the existence of such places is bound as a Christian man and a good citizen to do all in his power to suppress them, and thus coöperate with the Government. If existing legislation is not sufficient, let efforts be made to improve it.

Such are a few of the various ways in which wise legislation and the coöperation of society may aid in elevating its moral tone. But the Legislature does not attend to their cry;—who shall proclaim the wants of the other tens of thousands who do not make known their ignorance through their crime? It is the upper portion of society, bound to them by Christian sympathy, who should discover their need, comprehend the dreadful ignorance which exists in our land, and never cease from their personal efforts and their appeals for help, until such provision is made for them as was shown by the Lord's Committee so long ago to be needed, if the progress of crime in our country is to be arrested.

Not until then, not until all our children are educated, and the criminal class is brought under Christian influence, will the duty be fulfilled by society.

May all unite in this great work!

APPENDIX.

The following extracts from the last published Report of the Irish Convict Prisons show that the system is still working satisfactorily :—

" *Governor's Report of Spike Island Government Prisons.*

"No occurrence arose during the year to call for special notice or observation. All the able-bodied convicts, available for ordinary labour, were employed as heretofore on the docks in progress at Haulbowline Island, the greater portion being quarrying and stone dressing, and, I am happy to say, the Admiralty authorities, on their visit in September, appeared to be satisfied with the conduct of the men generally, and the manner in which they worked. In proof of this, His Excellency the Lord Lieutenant of Ireland, on the recommendation of the Lords of the Admiralty and Colonel Clarke, R.E., Director of Admiralty Works, was pleased to advance each convict one month in classification, which will have the effect of releasing them a month earlier. This boon on the part of His Excellency, being an approval of their conduct and industry, has been highly prized, and will, I feel sure, act as a stimulus to further exertions on their part.

Daily average number employed on the works
(prison works included) **657**
Not employed (in cells and hospital) **25**

Total daily average **682**

"The conduct of the convicts was generally satisfactory. There was no attempt at combination or
insubordinate conduct, except in individual cases.

" Corporal punishment was inflicted in five
instances, viz , in three cases of assaults on warders,
and two of general misconduct and refusing to work.

"I have had no intimation of any existing abuse
or abuses, and I have observed none ; there were no
attempts at escape.

" The buildings are in good order. Two divisions
of the prison are now in course of being subdivided
into separate cells, and when completed, the convicts,
when not at work, will be all kept in separation, and
I am confident that they will benefit by the change."

" *Lusk Intermediate Prison, January*, 1870.

" This is now the only Intermediate Prison, the
decrease in the number of skilled tradesmen, amongst
the convicts who qualified for Intermediate Prisons,
rendering the retention of Smithfield Prison, at a
very considerable annual cost, unnecessary ; accord-
ingly, in June last, the prisoners hitherto confined in
Smithfield were transferred to Lusk ; the services of

the entire Smithfield staff, with two exceptions, being no longer required, the remainder retired from the service upon pension, or receiving a gratuity, according to their length of service. The closing of Smithfield has not in any respect altered the positions of prisoners who are skilled tradesmen; all such cases have been employed at their respective trades at Lusk.

. "The closing of Smithfield Prison, rendering a re-arrangement of Lusk Prison staff necessary, Mr. Gunning, the Chief Warder of Lusk Prison, was appointed Superintendent, first-class Warder Daly, Steward and Registrar; and a slight addition made to the staff of subordinate officers.

"Dr. Quinlan and Mr. J. P. Organ retained their former appointments.

"The conduct of the subordinate officers has been satisfactory.

"The conduct of the prisoners has been very good; in three instances prisoners were removed to Mountjoy Male Prison for offences, none of which, however, were of a serious nature.

"No escape or attempt at escape took place during the year.

"The health of the prisoners has been good.

"During the past year, the farm has been partially fenced; a large barn has been built, and an iron hut taken down, and re-erected in a more suitable situation, by the prisoners."

" *Registrar and School Instructor's Report of Lusk Convict Prison.*

" On the 1st of January, 1869, there were in school of all classes 53 men, admitted during the year 106, making a total of 159 inmates within that period. Of these 89 were discharged, and 2 removed to Mountjoy Male Prison Hospital, leaving 68 inmates on 31st December, 1869.

" On looking over the school records I perceive that only two were discharged who could not read, and three who could not write their names, and these were men of such obtuse intellects that no teaching power could make any impression upon them. I have neither the right nor the inclination to ascribe to any merit of mine the educational advancement of the prisoners who pass through this prison, for, on their reception here, they have always shown the effects of careful attention in the prisons they had previously gone through ; and my best efforts are made to improve on the foundation laid for me. Many of the prisoners on their reception here have been so well educated that instructions from me would be superfluous, and cheerfully have they always given me their assistance in instructing their less favoured companions, and manifested their pleasure when they improved under their tuition. School instruction commences here each evening at half-past five o'clock, and terminates at half-past seven. The mode of instruction is just the same as it has been for the last twelve years, viz., reading, spelling, &c., writing on paper and on slates from dictation, arithmetic, simple lessons in grammar, and geography from maps. We have also exercises on the model ship, one evening in the week, and competitive examination on another. Instructions in letter-writing are given occasionally, and there is no subject in which the men take a greater interest than in this. I have the greatest pleasure in bearing my humble testimony to the admirable conduct of the prisoners; no sullenness, no discontent, no grumbling, but all alive to the advantages of the institution, and all harmoniously coöperating for its credit. When, towards the close of the year, it pleased the Almighty to remove from the field of his labour the late Mr. Organ—he who had been their kind preceptor for so many years—each man felt as if he had lost an individual friend, and all evinced the most sincere sorrow for his death. But the interest the men perceive to be taken in them for their future well-doing has given them renewed hope, and I have never known a better spirit to exist than does just now in Lusk Intermediate Convict Prison."

REVISED TABLE FOUNDED ON THE PENAL SERVITUDE ACT OF 1864.

Badge qualifying for Intermediate Prisons.	Sentences.	Shortest Periods of Imprisonment.		Longest Periods of Remission on License.	
		In Ordinary Prisons.	Shortest Period of detention in Intermediate Prisons		
		Yrs. Mths.	Yrs. Mths.	Yrs.	Mths.
13 A	5 years	3 — 5	0 — 6	1	1
21 A	6 "	4 — 1 (3—11)	0 — 7	1	4
29 A	7 "	4 — 9 (4—8)	0 — 8	1	7
37 A	8 "	5 — 5 (5—5)	0 — 9	1	10
53 A	10 "	6 — 9 (6—2)	0 — 11	2	4
69 A	12 "	8 — 1 (7—8)	1 — 1	1	10
93 A	15 "	10 — 1 (9—2 / 11—5)	1 — 4	3	7

The periods remitted on License will be proportionate to the length of sentences, and will depend upon the fitness of each Convict for release, after a careful consideration has been given to his case by the Government.

Table showing the Class or Number of Marks which it will be necessary for Female Prisoners convicted under the Penal Servitude Act, 27 & 28 Vic. Cap. 47 (July, 1864), to obtain, before becoming eligible for Licence in the Refuge, reckoning from the date of conviction.

Class and No. of Marks to be gained for Admission to the Refuges for different Sentences.	Sentences.	Shortest Periods of Imprisonment.		Earliest periods from termination of Sentence at which eligible for Licence to be passed, either in whole or part, at the Refuges.	
	Years.	Years.	Months.	Years.	Months.
Class 16 A or 16 months in A class ...	5	3	4	1	8
" 24 A " 24 "	6	4	0	2	0
" 32 A " 32 "	7	4	8	2	4
" 40 A " 40 "	8	5	4	2	8
" 56 A " 56 "	10	6	8	3	4
" 72 A " 72 "	12	8	0	4	0
" 96 A " 96 "	15	10	0	5	0

Extracts from the last Report of the Carlisle Memorial Refuge, Winchester, dated Dec. 31, 1871.

"It is now nearly seven years since this Refuge was established, for the reception, six months' prior to their liberation, of Female Convicts, whose conduct had proved satisfactory in the prisons. Under ordinary circumstances it would be unnecessary to dwell at any length upon the beneficial results which have been attained, because each annual report has shown that not only has due order been preserved in the Institution, but that beyond its walls, when the inmates have been subjected to the ordinary temptations of life, the fruits of their training, and of the friendly care and interest taken in their welfare, have been most satisfactorily manifested.

"An attempt has been made to furnish some reliable information with regard to those who have left the Refuge during the past three years—viz., 1869, 1870, and 1871 ; and in order to give to these statistics a special value — personal enquiries and visits have been made at their homes and places of employment, so far as was possible, by the Rev. Ashton Wells, who has kindly undertaken the management of the Institution, and by Miss Pumfrey, the Superintendent of the Refuge.

" The devotion of time and self-sacrifice required to prosecute these enquiries thoroughly and discreetly, can only be realised by those conversant with the criminal classes, who can also well appreciate the difference between *not being re-convicted*, and *known to be doing well.* Taking into consideration the class of persons dealt with, the great majority having been in crime from childhood, we might be very reasonably satisfied should a majority be returned under the former category. But our returns are still more favourable, and of such a nature as must prove entirely satisfactory both to the public, and to those who, at much sacrifice of time, money, and self, have taken such pains to procure them.

" During the three years 289 have been discharged, 33 have either been reconvicted, or their licences revoked.

" 21 have emigrated.

" 5 are known to have died.

" 25 lost knowledge of.

" 176 *ascertained to be doing well.*

" Of 29, although not re-convicted, from their associates and their manner of living, it has not been found possible to class them as doing well.

" Now although it has been thought desirable to give the statistics for three years, it must not be assumed that the enquiries have been limited to that period. Visits have been made to, and well authenticated communications received from, others who have left the Institution prior to the periods for which these returns are given.

" The books will show cases of persons in crime from 10 and 12 years of age, with as many as three penal servitude convictions registered against them, and with very outrageous and refractory prison conduct in the earlier stages of detention, who have since liberation lived many years in domestic service, under the constant observation of the authorities of the Refuge.

" There are so many of such cases that it is impossible to resist the conviction that by the exercise of untiring patience, zeal, and energy, more of this class can, under the blessing of God, be reclaimed, than those not conversant with the inner life of the criminal classes might deem possible.

" Miss Pumfrey has established an Emigration Class which promises extremely well, and has already been the means of assisting those who have relatives abroad, and wish to join them.

" The 'Emigration Class' is composed of volunteers for extra work in the Superintendent's room in the evenings, the proceeds of this extra work being devoted to assist emigration. It must not be supposed that the women who attend the 'Emigration Class' are confined to those desirous of emigrating, the brightest feature in it is, that there is a large attendance of those who have no intention of emigrating, but are actuated by the laudable desire of helping others.

" It is very creditable to the Superintendent that she is ready to devote her own time to this purpose, after the fatigues of the day. As the women are generally expected to make two shirts daily, the sacrifice which they make in working extra time may be duly estimated.

" With regard to work, although at one time it was very difficult to procure employment, the Institution has of late been better supplied, and it is to be hoped that this improved state of things may continue.

" It will be observed that a very large number have been placed in domestic service, their employers having been made aware of their antecedents. As many of these have again applied to the Institution for servants, it is impossible to produce better testimony to the success of the training.

" The objects of the Refuge have been much furthered by the lady visitors, and by the kindness of the Rev. C. Collier, who lectures periodically to the inmates on interesting and instructive subjects; as also by lecturers occasionally sent by the Temperance Association."

ARROWSMITH, PRINTER, 11 QUAY STREET, BRISTOL.

www.ingramcontent.com/pod-product-compliance
Lightning Source LLC
Chambersburg PA
CBHW020551270326
41927CB00006B/802